KT-179-115

THE
RECIPE
WHEEL

Louise,
Wishing you a very very
Happy 28th Birthday!
Lots of love
Charlie x x

THE
RECIPE WHEEL

ROSIE
RAMSDEN

EBURY
PRESS

FOR BADGE

1 3 5 7 9 10 8 6 4 2

Published in 2014 by Ebury Press, an imprint of Ebury Publishing

A Random House Group Company

Text © Rosie Ramsden 2014

Rosie Ramsden has asserted her right to be identified as the author of this Work in accordance with the Copyright, Designs and Patents Act 1988

All rights reserved. No part of this publication may be reproduced, stored in a retrieval system, or transmitted in any form or by any means, electronic, mechanical, photocopying, recording or otherwise, without the prior permission of the copyright owner.

The Random House Group Limited Reg. No. 954009

Addresses for companies within the Random House Group can be found at www.randomhouse.co.uk

A CIP catalogue record for this book is available from the British Library

The Random House Group Limited supports the Forest Stewardship Council® (FSC®), the leading international forest-certification organisation. Our books carrying the FSC label are printed on FSC®-certified paper. FSC is the only forest-certification scheme supported by the leading environmental organisations, including Greenpeace. Our paper procurement policy can be found at www.randomhouse.co.uk/environment

To buy books by your favourite authors and register for offers visit www.randomhouse.co.uk

Design: Will Webb
Illustrations: Rosie Ramsden

Printed and bound in China by C&C Offset Printing Co., Ltd

ISBN 978-0-09-195704-9

CONTENTS

Foreword

I like to draw and paint. Some days I paint fruit, some days vegetables; some days I draw mindless scribbles on Post-it notes. Scattered around my kitchen surfaces and marking pages in cookery books are torn bits of paper covered with scratchy mind maps, worn thin with coloured pen. It's the way I think about things. But mostly, it's what inspires me to cook.

This book follows the route of these doodled mind maps. It explores recipe ideas visually. Each chapter in this book has its own 'mind map' of sorts, its own recipe wheel. At the centre of each wheel lies a basic recipe and technique: bread; soup; risotto; roast chicken; braised beef; poached fish; gratin; wilted greens; sponge cake; custard. Nothing fancy. From these cores stem new, more developed ideas that all have the basic formula at their heart.

Each wheel puts a complete idea on to one page – no endless flicking through giant books or scrolling slow webpages – and draws on the simplicity of good, basic cooking. Recipes jump to varying levels of complexity and occasion, helping you decide what you really feel like making an effort with. Running along the spokes of the wheel are ways to help you choose what you want to cook. Select the dish you feel like by the length you want to go to – No Frills or Get Creative – or the occasion you're cooking for – Feeding Friends or Cooking to Impress. Make a different risotto for every month of the year, tart up your roast chicken to impress friends, and share the love using up your leftovers the day after. The wheels make it simple to adapt recipes, substitute ingredients and play with flavours according to your mood.

Deciding what to cook can sometimes take hours – sometimes it comes naturally and you have a culinary brainwave – but I do enjoy the time spent thinking about it. There are a few key things that I bear in mind when building up a recipe.

The first is balance. Make sure there is a good balance of flavours and textures in the dish – sweet, savoury, crunchy, smooth, salty and sour. Bitter things love sweetness, and you can balance salt with a squeeze of sour citrus or something acidic. Cream soothes spice, but can often enrich blandness. Salt greatly enhances flavour – add it at the beginning and just at the end of cooking. And always have herbs at hand to freshen up leftovers.

The second is colour. We're lucky in the UK that each season brings with it a rainbow of colours that can liven up the way your food looks in the dish. I'm not saying that food has to look good to taste good, but it makes cooking and eating more fun. Vegetables and fruit are where most of the colour comes from, and it's purple veg that excites me most. Radicchio, beetroot, radishes, rhubarb. And for fruit, dark plums, figs, blackberries and cherries. Mix these into green and yellow and you'll have a plate that looks and tastes beautiful.

The third is leftovers. Leftovers form an important part of this book and of many of my wheels – and all of us have them. They are strange and wonderful things to work with, frugal, inventive and often surprising. Some of the recipe wheel ideas use the leftover core as their base. It's when you eat leftovers that you discover that some things taste much better the next day. Transformational.

This is chiefly a book about loving and understanding the food you cook. It's about discovering what you like and how to get there. And I encourage you to draw or imagine your own wheels. Start with the basics, and move forward to something a little different; or go on a wild tangent, knowing that you'll never stray too far away from what you already know.

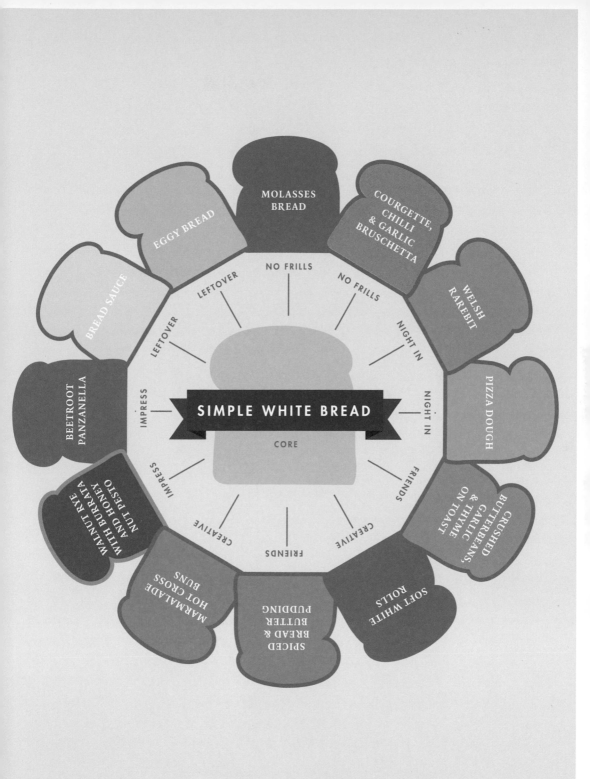

Simple White Bread

The bread wheel divides itself between recipes for fresh loaves and recipes for leftover loaves. It urges home bread-making and explores the fruitfulness of stale bread.

Making bread is an age-old therapy. The mixing of yeast with flour and water into a dough, kneading and watching it rise to double its size, is creative and calming – and every time you do it, it gets easier, and tastier. It is this that excites me most: starting with practically nothing, and ending up with something that forms the basis of so many recipes.

Its short lifespan holds a great deal of opportunity: spread a fresh slice with butter; toast another and smother it with crushed, cooked beans; soak it, slightly stale, in creamy custard and bake; soften it in oil for salads; or crumble it, dry, on top of bubbling gratins. Knead, rest, bake, rest, slice, dunk, spread, whiz.

Knead to know. Notes on bread.

- Mixing your bread with anything that's much hotter than lukewarm (35–45°C) will kill the yeast and stop it leavening the dough. Any warmer than 50°C and the cells in the yeast start to die.

- Salt is also a yeast-attacker. Make sure you activate your yeast with a little warm water before it mixes with the dough, and keep the salt to one side of your flour as you make a well so it doesn't mix in straight away.

- Slow down your bread-making process by letting the dough rise in the fridge – this is called retarding. When I'm short of time, I make the dough at lunchtime, knead it, let it rise in the fridge until the evening, knead it again, shape it, and put it back in the fridge overnight for a second rise. In the morning, I bake.

- Throw a glassful of water into the oven while you bake to create steam – this will help to form a good crust.

- Check your loaf is done by tapping it on the bottom to see whether it sounds hollow. If you're still not sure if the loaf is ready, stick a digital thermometer into its centre – if it reaches an internal temperature somewhere between 80°C and 100°C it's good to come out of the oven and cool.

- A good way to keep loaves fresh is to wrap them in clingfilm. Leaving them out will turn them stale more quickly. Toasting and soaking stale bread for salads and soups remedies all. You can freeze loaves, freshly baked, then defrost them.

Simple white bread

CORE

Good bread doesn't hang around long in our house – we spread marmalade thickly on it for breakfast, dip it in soup for lunch and make crostini for dinner. All that's left are a few odds and ends. This core bread recipe is so easy to whip up that, once you've got it nailed, you'll be making it every weekend and finding fresh, meandering ways to get the best out of it. Using strong white bread flour for baking is very forgiving – it's made up of proteins and starch that help the yeast to activate and your dough to rise.

You can easily double the ingredients to make two loaves. Freeze one or half a loaf if you're not going to eat it all over the next few days. It's always tempting to crack into the loaf still warm, but it's worth waiting until it has completely cooled for the perfect texture.

1 x 7g sachet of fast-action dried yeast
    (I use Allinson)
200ml lukewarm water
300g strong white bread flour, plus extra
    for dusting
50g wholemeal bread flour
1 tablespoon fine sea salt
olive oil, for greasing

MAKES	TIME TO MIX & KNEAD	TIME TO COOK
1 SMALL LOAF	20 MINUTES + PROVING	40–50 MINUTES

1. Mix the yeast with 2 tablespoons of the warm water and set aside in a warm place for 10 minutes to fizz and froth.

2. Sift the flours together into a large bowl and sprinkle the salt to one side. Push the flour to the sides of the bowl to form a well in the centre, making space to pour in the liquid. Pour in the warm yeast mixture with the rest of the warm water and slowly fold in the flours with your hands. (Fly off the path and add walnuts, raisins, pumpkin seeds or olives here.)

3. When the mixture is combined into a sticky but manageable dough, turn it out on to a lightly oiled surface. Using the heel of your hand and your knuckles, knead the dough by pulling it towards you, pushing it away and folding it back in. Do this for 10 minutes, until the dough feels soft and begins to bounce back when you press it with a finger.

4. Place the springy dough in a lightly oiled bowl, loosely cover with clingfilm, and set aside to prove for 1 hour in a warm – but not too hot – place, or overnight in the fridge, until it has almost doubled in size.

5. Bring the dough back on to the oiled surface and knead again for another 5 minutes. Shape the dough into a ball by gently folding the sides of the dough under itself. Transfer the dough to a lightly floured baking tray or loaf tin, folds facing down, and leave to prove, loosely covered, for another 30 minutes, until risen again.

6. Preheat the oven to 230°C/fan 210°C/gas 8. When the dough has had time to prove and rise once more, score a few lines into the top using a very sharp serrated knife or a Stanley blade. Lightly dust the top of the dough with plain flour, then slide it into the oven. Throw a glassful of water into the bottom of the oven and shut the door so that the steam rises up and over the loaf to form a crust.

7. Bake for 40–50 minutes, until a golden crust has formed and the bread appears hollow – you can test this by knocking on the underside of the loaf or by checking the inner temperature with a thermometer (see tips, page 11). It should sound like you are tapping on the sole of an empty shoe.

8. Transfer the loaf to a wire rack and leave it to cool completely – the loaf keeps on cooking as it cools – before slicing.

Molasses bread

This bread makes great toast as soon as it goes a little stale, giving you an outrageous combination of sticky, sweet and crisp. Spread it thickly with Marmite, caramelise it for brown bread ice cream, or slather it with smoked salmon, beetroot and soured cream.

Wholewheats absorb water in a different way from white bread flour, which means you may need to add more liquid to your dough. The more wholewheat flour you use, the more water you'll need. The dough will feel gummy and be less manageable to knead, but will produce a much better crumb. Add the water a little at a time so you can judge how easy your dough is to handle. To give more rise to a wholewheat dough, or to make it easier to wield, blend it with strong white flour. A pure wholewheat loaf will be smaller but just as delicious.

Adding a little bit of dark molasses sugar adds starch to your wholemeal flour and gives a smooth caramel flavour while also kicking the yeast into action.

1 x 7g sachet of fast-action dried yeast
(I use Allinson)
250ml lukewarm water
3 tablespoons loose molasses sugar
250g strong wholemeal bread flour
100g strong white bread flour
1 tablespoon fine sea salt
olive oil, for greasing

MAKES	TIME TO MIX & KNEAD	TIME TO COOK
1 SMALL LOAF	25 MINUTES + PROVING	40–50 MINUTES

1. Mix the yeast with 2 tablespoons of the warm water and the sugar and set aside in a warm place for 10 minutes to fizz and froth. Sift the flours together into a large bowl and sprinkle the salt to one side. Push the flour to the sides of the bowl to form a well in the centre. Pour in the warm yeast mixture and slowly fold in the flours and sugar with your hands. Add the remaining warm water a little at a time so you can manage its texture – it will be wet, so be prepared to get a little sticky.

2. Once combined, bring the dough on to a lightly oiled surface to knead. Knead it by pulling it towards you, pushing it away and folding it back in with the heel of your hand. Do this for 10 minutes, until the dough feels soft and begins to bounce back when you press it with a finger. It will feel more dense than a white bread dough. Alternatively, knead the dough in a stand mixer fitted with the dough hook.

3. Place the dough in a lightly oiled bowl, loosely cover with clingfilm, then set aside for 1–2 hours in a warm place or overnight in the fridge until it has almost doubled in size.

4. Bring the dough back on to an oiled surface and knead again for another 5 minutes. Gently form it into a ball shape, gently folding the sides of the dough under itself. Replace in the oiled bowl, folds facing down, and leave to prove for another hour.

5. Preheat the oven to 230°C/fan 210°C/gas 8. When the dough has had time to prove and rise, gently tip it, without knocking the air out, on to a floured baking tray, and score the top of the dough a few times with a very sharp knife or a Stanley blade. Slide into the oven. Throw a glassful of water into the bottom of the oven to help a good crust develop and shut the door. Bake for 40–50 minutes, until golden and the bread is cooked – you can test this by knocking on the underside of the loaf or by checking the inner temperature with a thermometer (see tips, page 11). Transfer to a wire rack and leave to cool completely before slicing.

Courgette, chilli and garlic bruschetta

NO FRILLS

Just-charred, two-day-old white bread rubbed with peppery garlic and topped with juicy courgettes is one idea that never seems to disappoint. Next time, marinate super-ripe tomatoes with a little sugar, salt and olive oil and serve simply with a toasted white loaf. Or, following exactly the same method, char thinly sliced asparagus spears or artichoke hearts, toss them with chopped fresh parsley or tarragon, lay them on the toasts and scatter over grated pecorino.

1 large or 2 small courgettes

grated zest and juice of 1 lemon

½ or 1 red chilli, finely chopped (taste your chilli first to see how hot it is – you don't want to blow up the dish)

4 slightly stale slices from a large round loaf, halved

1 clove of garlic, crushed

extra virgin olive oil, for drizzling

a few fresh basil leaves

1. Thinly shave the courgettes with a vegetable peeler and toss in a small bowl with the lemon zest and juice and the chilli. Season well with sea salt and black pepper.

2. Toast the bread on a hot griddle pan for 3 minutes on each side, so that it begins to char. Find the plate you want to serve your bruschetta on (if they get that far...), then remove the bread from the griddle, rub the top with garlic, and drizzle with olive oil. Set aside.

3. Throw the courgettes into the hot griddle pan and fry for 3 minutes, until wilted and juicy. Using tongs, or a slotted spoon, top the toasted bread with the courgettes, reserving any leftover juices for dressings, and serve with a few leaves of basil.

MAKES

8 SLICES

READY IN

20 MINUTES

Welsh rarebit

Rarebit perks up old bread (and tired heads) no end. It has the gooiness and stale bread revivingness of your average cheese on toast – so long as we're talking mustard and a bucketload of cheese – but with added spice, salt and booze. Strong, good-quality Cheddar is needed here, and it's worth seeking out a powerful one, as this is the main event of the recipe. No tiptoeing around ... As your teeth sink in, you want to feel a blast of heat and minimal difference in texture between topping and bread base.

4 tablespoons stout (Meantime London stout has a good flavour)
1 tablespoon Worcestershire sauce
1 tablespoon English mustard
a couple of drops of Tabasco
1 large free-range egg yolk
125g strong vintage Cheddar cheese (such as Lincolnshire Poacher or a good salty aged Cheddar – Keen's and Montgomery's are both good)
4 slices of simple white bread or slices from a large round loaf

1. In a saucepan, mix together the stout, Worcestershire sauce, mustard and Tabasco and set over a low heat. Whisk in the egg yolk and add the cheese, stirring as it slowly melts and becomes a thick paste. Take it off the heat. If the cheese starts to seize and split it's because it has heated up too quickly and formed clumps. Go slow.

2. Meanwhile, lightly toast the bread on both sides under the grill. Remove and spread thickly with the cheese mixture. Put the toasts under the grill again and cook for 5 minutes, until golden and bubbling. Cool slightly, then serve.

MAKES

4 TOASTS

READY IN

15 MINUTES

Pizza dough

This dough is flexible, smooth and fun to play with – press it with your fingertips, bash it, fold it and throw it around the tabletop. Using finely ground Tipo '00' flour gives a more elastic dough, making it easier to stretch, though you can also use strong white bread flour. Sandy semolina clings to the base and crisps just enough for crunch and chew, while soaking up the juices of the topping to give way to a doughy droop that moves your head to your chin to catch it. The best party food, knocked up in no time.

Freeze the dough at the stage just before you roll it out – it will keep in the freezer for up to 3 months – and defrost to continue with the recipe.

1 x 7g sachet of fast-action dried yeast
    (I use Allinson)
½ tablespoon golden caster sugar
2 tablespoons extra virgin olive oil
300ml lukewarm water
500g Tipo '00' flour or strong white bread flour
1 teaspoon fine sea salt
50g finely ground semolina flour

MAKES

4 LARGE PIZZAS

TIME TO MIX & KNEAD

20 MINUTES + PROVING

TIME TO COOK

15 MINUTES

1. Mix the yeast, sugar, oil and half the lukewarm water together and set aside for 10 minutes to fizz and froth. Combine the flour and salt together in a bowl and make a well in the centre. Pour the yeast mix and the rest of the warm water into the well and gradually beat in the flour with a fork, until the dough starts to come together. Knead in the bowl for 5–10 minutes, until the dough is soft and elastic. Cover the bowl with clingfilm and leave to rise in a warm place for an hour, until almost doubled in size.

2. Knock the dough back on a lightly oiled surface and roll it into 4 little balls. You can wrap it in clingfilm at this stage and either leave it in the fridge for up to 3 hours, until ready to use, or freeze it, defrost and allow to rise for use another day.

3. Preheat the oven to 180°C/fan 160°C/gas 4. Scatter the table with the semolina. Flatten each ball of dough into a circle, pressing it out with your fingertips, and stretch with a rolling pin into 4 x 0.5cm thick circles. Use a 20cm cake tin base as a guide if you like. Oddly shaped pizzas are fun too.

4. Place the rolled dough on an oiled piece of foil or a floured baking sheet, spread thinly with tomato and add your favourite toppings (see page 20). Slide on to a baking tray and bake for 15 minutes, until the edges and base of the pizzas are crisp.

5 utterly luscious pizza toppings:

- Add thinly sliced lardo or pancetta, blanched and squeezed chard, chopped red chilli and a generous grating of Parmesan.

- Mix capers and chopped anchovy into torn mozzarella and scatter over the pizza topping liberally. Best served tomato-free.

- Spread a light-tasting tomato passata on to the pizza base, grate over smoked ricotta with mozzarella if you like, and scatter small bits of creamy 'nduja over the top. Add rocket after baking.

- Blanch kale, squeeze out the extra juices and add to a tomato and mozzarella pizza. Crack an egg in the middle and bake. Drizzle with chilli oil.

- For more of a tear and share side, dollop pesto on to a white pizza base and scatter with Parmesan and garlic oil. Season generously and bake.

Crushed butter beans, garlic and thyme on toast

These ingredients were made for each other, and it's a simple combination, so you can play with it. Try it on rye bread; rosemary and parsley go well too; use borlotti beans next time; and it doesn't matter how well you mash the beans, a bit of texture does no harm. You can easily halve this amount but 20 toasts will go down pretty quickly.

2 x 400g tins of butter beans, drained and well rinsed
100ml olive oil, plus extra for drizzling
2 cloves of garlic, sliced
2 sprigs of fresh thyme, leaves removed and stalks discarded
2 tablespoons single cream
10 slices from a round loaf, halved

1. Heat the butter beans with 2 tablespoons of water in a medium saucepan over a medium-high heat for 2–3 minutes, until you can just squash them with the back of a spoon. Pour off any water that has not been absorbed and add a little oil to the pan with the garlic. Then turn down the heat and cook gently for another 2 minutes.

2. Pour the butter bean mix into a food processor with half the thyme leaves and the cream. Pulse, gradually pouring in the rest of the oil, until you have a rough but creamy paste. Season well with salt and pepper. You can use a potato masher to do this too.

3. Toast your bread under the grill until crisp and golden. Transfer the toast to plates or a board and thickly spread with the butter beans. Top with the remaining thyme leaves, drizzle with olive oil and serve.

MAKES ENOUGH FOR

20 TOASTS

READY IN

15 MINUTES

Soft white rolls

A quick snap in the oven allows just enough time for the dough to puff and form a light crust. Tear open the buns when cooled to find fluffy, creamy white centres – helped along by the addition of milk and butter. They're perfect for stuffing with the day's lunch or lashings of bacon. Otherwise, top each bun with sesame seeds before they go into the oven, and you'll have a cemita ready for filling (see braised beef, page 124).

50ml lukewarm water
75ml lukewarm whole milk
25g unsalted butter, melted
1 x 7g sachet of fast-action dried yeast
    (I use Allinson)
½ teaspoon runny honey
350g strong white bread flour,
    plus extra for dusting
2 teaspoons fine sea salt

MAKES

4 ROLLS

TIME TO MIX & KNEAD

25 MINUTES + PROVING

TIME TO COOK

15–20 MINUTES

1. Mix the warm water and milk, butter, yeast and honey together in a bowl and set aside for 10 minutes to fizz and froth. Sift the flour into a large bowl and make a well, sprinkling the salt to one side. Pour in the yeast mixture and begin to fold in the flour, using your hands. When the mixture is combined into a sticky dough, turn it out on to a lightly oiled surface. Knead the dough by pulling it towards you, pushing it away and folding it back in with the heel of your hand and your knuckles. Do this for 5 minutes, until the dough feels soft and pliable.

2. Place the dough in a lightly oiled bowl, loosely cover with lightly oiled clingfilm, and set aside for 1 hour in a warm, humid, cosy place or overnight in the fridge until it has almost doubled in size.

3. Bring the dough back on to a floured surface and knead again for another 5 minutes. Roll into a large ball and cut into quarters, then roll each one into a ball shape. Space out the 4 dough balls evenly on a lightly oiled tray. Loosely cover with clingfilm and leave to rise again for 30 minutes.

4. While the dough is resting, preheat the oven to 230°C/fan 210°C/gas 8. Dust the rolls with flour, then slide the tray into the oven. Bake for 15–20 minutes, until puffed up and golden. Transfer the rolls to a wire rack and leave to cool completely before slicing.

Spiced bread and butter pudding

Drown bread in cream, then bake it. Let it crisp and ooze and squelch under your spoon. Bread and butter pudding halts conversation at the dinner table, only to be interrupted by snuffles and grunts – the good kind. If you're using fresh bread, the custard won't soak up completely and will leave you with a runnier b & b – though that may be what you like. Staler bread is much more absorbent, due to its lower moisture content, and will produce a far more spongy pudding. I sometimes leave the crusts on – texture rules this dish.

300g simple white bread, 3–4 days old, crusts removed, sliced in half to make triangles

50g softened unsalted butter

30g sultanas, soaked in 20ml warmed golden rum for 20 minutes to plump them up

50g chopped hazelnuts

1 medium free-range egg, plus 2 egg yolks

200ml whole milk

200ml double cream

75g caster sugar

½ teaspoon ground cinnamon

¼ teaspoon ground cloves

2 tablespoons dark rum (optional)

grated zest of ½ a lemon

a pinch of flaked sea salt

granulated sugar, for sprinkling

SERVES

4–6

TIME TO PREPARE

20 MINUTES

TIME TO COOK

40 MINUTES

1. Lightly grease a 1 litre ovenproof dish or loaf tin, or something large enough to tower the sliced bread – bearing in mind that it will swell as it soaks. Butter the bread on both sides and lay one-third of the slices, side by side, in the bottom of the dish. Sprinkle with one-third of the rum-soaked sultanas and the hazelnuts. Repeat this until you have used up all the ingredients.

2. In a large measuring jug, whisk the egg and egg yolks. Mix in the milk and cream, then add the sugar, spices and rum (if using). When well mixed, pour over the bread, pressing the top layer down into the cream mix to coat. Set the dish aside for 30 minutes so that the bread soaks up some of the liquid.

3. Set the oven to 180°C/fan 160°C/gas 4. Sprinkle the top of the pudding with sugar, then place in the oven and bake for 40 minutes, until the top bread layer is golden and crisp. Best served with a wobble and a generous drizzle of single cream. Pretty good cold too.

Marmalade hot cross buns

GET CREATIVE

Hot cross buns have more chew than a simple bread roll, and are sweeter too, but their methods are not too dissimilar. Adding a few ingredients can turn breakfast into something more like teatime. The sticky marmalade is an extra – it goes well with spices and orange zest, but is not altogether necessary. Use no-bits marmalade if you like, or opt for apricot jam, honey or a little sugar syrup, made by simmering equal parts sugar and water until clear, uncoloured and sticky. If you're keen on bitter citrus, though, try adding a little marmalade to the dough too.

1 x 7g sachet of fast-action dried yeast
 (I use Allinson)
50g caster sugar
150ml lukewarm whole milk
450g strong white bread flour
2 teaspoons mixed spice
1 teaspoon fine sea salt
1 large free-range egg, lightly beaten
grated zest of 1 orange
2 tablespoons runny honey
150g currants or raisins
thin-cut marmalade, to glaze (see introduction)

FOR THE CROSS
35g plain flour
1 tablespoon sunflower oil
30ml water

MAKES	TIME TO MIX & KNEAD	TIME TO COOK
8 BUNS	**25** MINUTES + PROVING	**15–20** MINUTES

1. Mix the yeast in a bowl with the sugar and lukewarm milk and leave for 10 minutes to froth. Sift the flour and spice into a large bowl, sprinkling the salt to one side. Lightly beat together the egg, orange zest, honey and currants until combined. Make a well in the flour and pour in the yeast mix and the egg mixture. Fold in the flour with your hands to make a soft dough. If it's too wet and sticky to manage, add a little more flour; if too dry, add a drop more lukewarm milk.

2. Allow to rest for 10 minutes, then knead, briefly, on a lightly oiled surface, pulling the dough away from you and pushing it with the heel of your hand and your knuckles. Sit the dough in a lightly oiled bowl, cover with a floured tea towel or lightly oiled clingfilm, and place in a warm spot for 1 hour to prove, or overnight in the fridge.

3. Cut the dough into 8 equal-sized pieces, roll them into balls, and lay them in lines on a large, floured baking sheet, leaving a three-finger-sized gap between. Leave to prove for 20–30 minutes, covered with a floured tea towel or lightly oiled clingfilm, until almost doubled in size.

4. Preheat the oven to 230°C/fan 210°C/gas 8. To make the cross, mix together the flour, oil and water. Spoon the dough into a disposable piping bag (you can buy these from cook shops and online – always handy …) with a small round nozzle and squeeze 2 thin lines over the buns to make a cross. It should stretch easily over the buns to form a cross. Alternatively, drape the mixture over the buns with a spoon. Slide the buns into the oven to bake for 15–20 minutes, until puffed, golden and hollow-sounding when knocked. The inner temperature should reach about 85–88°C (see tips, page 11).

5. Remove to a wire rack and glaze with plenty of marmalade while still warm. Cut in half, toast under the grill and smother with softened butter.

Walnut rye with burrata and honey nut pesto

Rye flour gives this loaf a tight, dense crumb and a sharp, nutty flavour. When you realise that your rye won't be a pillowy and light loaf but a dark and crumbly one, you'll start to love it even more for its complex, unique flavour. It tastes and feels virtuous, but is by no means lifeless. It's even better toasted. Spreading it with creamy burrata (buffalo mozzarella mixed with cream) and nutty pesto is such a marvellous way to serve it.

Like a wholemeal loaf, the more rye flour you use, the more water you need. It will be sticky but will produce a much moister loaf – if it's too wet to handle, use a dough hook on a stand mixer to knead. I've lightened the mixture, here, by adding a little white flour.

Walnut rye makes a great sourdough loaf too. It makes a tightly packed, wet dough with an acidity that is delicious with the sweet pesto. If you have a sourdough starter, replace the yeast and warm water with 100g of starter and mix with the flour, adding enough water just to bind.

FOR THE RYE
1 x 7g sachet of fast-action dried yeast
    (I use Allinson)
200–250ml lukewarm water
1 tablespoon loose molasses sugar
175g rye bread flour
50g wholemeal bread flour
75g strong white bread flour
1 teaspoon fine sea salt
a handful of chopped walnuts
olive oil, for greasing

FOR THE HONEY WALNUTS
AND BURRATA
100g chopped walnuts
50g grated Parmesan cheese
75ml olive oil
4 tablespoons runny honey
a small handful of fresh thyme, leaves picked
1–2 fresh balls of burrata (available from Whole
    Foods, Waitrose, Italian delis and good cheese
    mongers – if you can't get hold of burrata, use
    a good-quality buffalo mozzarella or ricotta)

1. Mix the yeast with 2 tablespoons of the lukewarm water and the molasses sugar and set aside for 10 minutes to bubble and froth. Sift the flours into a bowl and make a well in the centre, sprinkling the salt to one side. Pour the frothy yeast into the well and gradually mix in the walnuts and the flour with your hands, adding the rest of the water drop by drop as you mix – you want it sticky, as the flour will absorb the water while it rests. Leave the dough to rest for 10 minutes.

2. Knead the dough on a lightly oiled surface for 10 minutes – get sticky! – adding a little more oil to the surface if needed. Return the dough to a lightly oiled bowl and leave for 1 hour, until risen by half.

3. Knead briefly. Lightly grease and flour a 1kg loaf tin and shape the dough to fit snugly inside. Leave to rise for a second time until risen by half again.

4. Preheat the oven to 230°C/fan 210°C/gas 8. Place the loaf in the oven and bake for 50 minutes to 1 hour, until baked through, checking its inner temperature with a thermometer (see page 11) or knocking for a hollow sound. Remove from the oven and leave in its tin to cool slightly. Then tip out on to a wire rack to cool completely before slicing.

5. Meanwhile, make the pesto. Grind the walnuts and Parmesan together in a food processor or a pestle and mortar to a fine breadcrumb consistency. Season with salt and black pepper, then, still whizzing, slowly pour in the olive oil until the walnuts have formed a paste. Spoon into a bowl and stir in the honey. Top with the thyme leaves. Spread generously on the rye bread with the burrata.

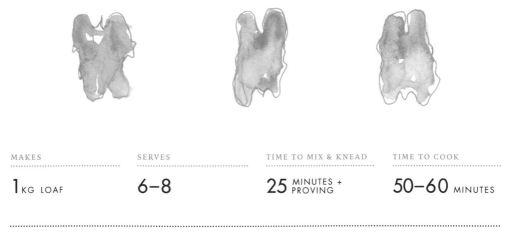

MAKES	SERVES	TIME TO MIX & KNEAD	TIME TO COOK
1 KG LOAF	6–8	25 MINUTES + PROVING	50–60 MINUTES

Beetroot panzanella

COOK TO IMPRESS

There is something weirdly good about soggy bread. It sounds wrong, but staleness can be the perfect sponge for liquids and, in this case, flavour. Here, the juices from beetroots, orange and ripe tomatoes are soaked up to give an old loaf a new lease of life. Harking back to other panzanella recipes – originally a Florentine way of using bread in salad – the bread is squeezed dry after being dressed, but I like it with all the juices locked in.

2 tablespoons red wine vinegar
1½ teaspoons granulated sugar
juice of ½ an orange
1 clove of garlic, crushed
50ml extra virgin olive oil, plus extra for drizzling
175g white bread or sourdough, slightly stale,
    crusts removed, cut into 2cm cubes
1 tablespoon capers, drained and rinsed
¼ of a red onion, very thinly sliced
10 very ripe baby plum/cherry tomatoes,
    deseeded and roughly chopped
2 large purple and candy (if you can find it)
    beetroot (about 400g), cut into wedges
a large handful of fresh basil leaves

SERVES

4

TIME TO PREPARE

20 MINUTES

TIME TO COOK

40–50 MINUTES

1. To make the dressing, mix together the red wine vinegar, sugar, orange juice and garlic, then slowly whisk in the olive oil. Season well with salt and pepper. Add the bread, capers, onion and tomatoes and set aside to absorb while you prepare the beetroot. It can stay like this for a few hours, covered, in the fridge.

2. Preheat the oven to 200°C/fan 180°C/gas 6. Lay a sheet of foil in a roasting tin and add the beetroot. Season with salt and pepper and drizzle with olive oil. Tightly fold the foil around the beetroot and slide into the oven. Roast for 40–50 minutes, until tender and juicy. Test the tenderness by piercing with a knife – you'll feel if the middle is still hard. If it is, put it back in for another 10 minutes or so. Remove from the oven and leave to cool, then peel off the skin. Reserve the juices.

3. Remove the dressed bread from the fridge and transfer to a large platter. Place the beetroot around the salad, without mixing so that the purple juices don't stain the other ingredients, and drizzle with a little of the beetroot roasting juices. Top with whole or torn basil leaves and serve with barbecued or grilled meat.

Another stale bread salad

For another stale bread salad, fattoush, toast pieces of stale pitta – or any other bread – in a hot pan with olive oil until crisp and golden. Make a dressing in the bottom of a large bowl, whisking 1 tablespoon of red wine vinegar, a pinch of sugar, a good squeeze of lemon juice and 3 tablespoons of extra virgin olive oil. Add the pitta to the bowl of dressing and toss in chopped fresh parsley, dill, mint and coriander, very finely sliced onions, small black Kalamata olives, ripe tomatoes, quartered, and a good pinch of lemony sumac. Drizzle over more olive oil to serve.

Bread sauce

A bizarre bready porridge. No Sunday roast can be without it. Make it thinner than you think you'd like it – it'll thicken as it stands.

500ml whole milk

1 onion, peeled, halved and studded with 4 cloves

a good grating of nutmeg

2 bay leaves

½ a loaf of simple white bread (200g), slightly stale

25g butter

1. Put the milk into a pan with the clove-studded onion, nutmeg and bay leaves and gently bring to the boil. Remove from the heat and allow the hot milk to infuse with the spices for 10 minutes. Strain through a sieve into a clean pan and set back on the heat to simmer for 5 minutes. Remove from the heat.

2. Meanwhile, slice the crusts off the bread and tear the bread into 2.5cm chunks. Gradually stir them into the milk, then add the butter. You want it to have a gooey, spongy consistency. Season well with salt and pepper and serve. Dollop on the side of your roast chicken, and douse with gravy. It's even better the next day.

MAKES

700G

READY IN

30 MINUTES

Eggy bread

Use 4-day-old bread. The staleness of the bread soaks up the egg and milk, swells and holds its shape. Eggy bread makes a superb breakfast, speedy lunch or Sunday night supper. Add a sliced green chilli to the beaten egg for punch, or for sweet French toast dust with a tablespoon each of ground cinnamon and icing sugar, then serve with crispy bacon and drizzle with maple syrup.

8 medium free-range eggs, lightly beaten
2 tablespoons whole milk
a good pinch of cayenne pepper
4 thick slices of simple white bread, slightly stale, or a large round loaf, crusts removed
a knob of butter

1. In a large bowl, mix the eggs and milk with the cayenne pepper. Season generously with sea salt and plenty of black pepper. Dip the sliced bread in the egg mix and leave to absorb for 20 minutes.

2. Melt the butter in a large pan or on a griddle. Fry the eggy bread for 5 minutes on each side, until golden and crisp but still slightly gooey in the middle.

MAKES

4 THICK SLICES

READY IN

30 MINUTES

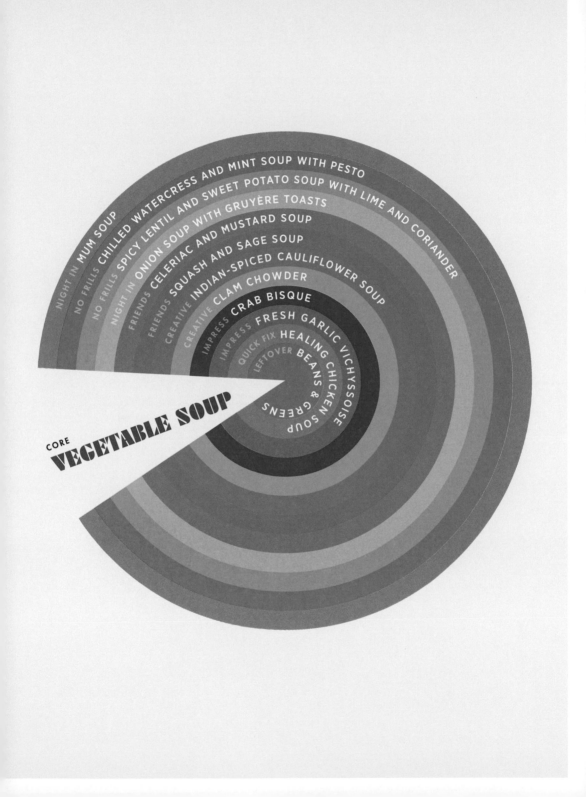

NIGHT IN MUM SOUP

NO FRILLS CHILLED WATERCRESS AND MINT SOUP WITH PESTO

NO FRILLS SPICY LENTIL AND SWEET POTATO SOUP WITH LIME AND CORIANDER

NIGHT IN ONION SOUP WITH GRUYÈRE TOASTS

FRIENDS CELERIAC AND MUSTARD SOUP

FRIENDS SQUASH AND SAGE SOUP

CREATIVE INDIAN-SPICED CAULIFLOWER SOUP

CREATIVE CLAM CHOWDER

IMPRESS CRAB BISQUE

IMPRESS FRESH GARLIC VICHYSSOISE

QUICK FIX HEALING CHICKEN SOUP

LEFTOVER BEANS & GREENS

CORE VEGETABLE SOUP

Vegetable Soup

Just picturing a ladle curling out of a giant soup pot and watching steam breeze from a deep bowl conjures up some of the best food feelings in me. With every soup I make or eat there is always a sense that I'm being brought back to health. Even saying the word 'soup' is a tonic. Soup, whether it's a healthy concoction or not, is remedial, medicinal and feel-good. And, more than anything, it's incredibly easy to make.

The simplest of soups makes the base to this chapter: a not-too-precise gathering of ingredients that, when fried until soft, stewed and simmered, make the most satisfying of lunches. This core recipe is simple to build on – take bits you want to experiment with, or nuggets which need using up, stir them in and go from there. Make your soup clear, chilled, chunky or smooth, all from the same formula.

Sweat the vegetables for as long as they can take it before browning – you want them buttery, softened, well-seasoned and jammed with flavour. If you can find it, use good fresh stock. Sometimes the herby stock pots are a little overwhelming for delicate flavours, so, if using, dilute only half a pot for a soup to feed 4. In all these soup recipes, the butter can be swapped for olive oil – though it won't have as creamy a flavour.

Tips for splendid soup

- Water can be used in place of stock – it will give a lovely, clean flavour to the soup if the vegetables are cooked for long enough with enough seasoning and if the soup is simmered for at least 45 minutes. Some ready-made stocks can be very salty, so taste before seasoning. In any case, a quick season before you serve always brings out flavour.

- If adding wine to soup, make sure you simmer it for at least 5 minutes before adding stock, otherwise it can make the soup taste harshly acidic.

- Think about what you garnish a soup with. Pair your soup with opposing flavours and textures to jazz up the soup: go crunchy for smooth soups, like croutons, or spring onions; put salty things on top of sweet soups, like pancetta on pea soup; fresh herbs on heavy soups; and smooth things on chunky soups, like soured cream or yoghurt.

Vegetable soup

This is a no-frills soup and, while being a launchpad for other potages, it can hold its own wonderfully. Sometimes I fill the bowl with fresh herbs just as I serve it, or stir a pinch of chilli flakes into the vegetables as they fry for a little kick. Treat it as a bare canvas.

If serving this soup as is, it's worth keeping it unblended. You want a clean taste, and to be able to enjoy everything that has gone into it rather than merging it into one flavour. Cook slow and low for the best results.

a good knob of unsalted butter
1 large onion, finely chopped
1 large stick of celery, washed and finely chopped
2 carrots, peeled and finely chopped
2 bay leaves
leaves from 1 sprig of fresh thyme
1 large waxy potato, peeled and roughly chopped
     (waxy potatoes hold their shape better –
     use floury ones if intending to blend)
1.5 litres chicken or vegetable stock, or water

1. Melt the butter in a large saucepan over a low heat, then add the onion, celery, carrot and herbs. Season well and gently fry, covered, for 10–15 minutes, until the vegetables are buttery and soft but not browned. You want to make a flavoursome base for the liquid you're about to put in.

2. Add the potato and fry for another 2 minutes. Pour in the stock, then cover and bring to the boil. Gently simmer for about 45 minutes, until the vegetables are tender and the broth is sweet and buttery. Season to taste and serve.

SERVES

4

TIME TO PREPARE

15 MINUTES

TIME TO COOK

1 HOUR

Mum soup

Packed full of vegetables and pulses, Mum soup – my mum's recipe from her mum – has always been my go-to recipe when it comes to beating ferocious colds, overcoming sheer hunger or easing hangovers. After making Mum soup once or twice, the recipe is unforgettable. The best thing is, you can throw all the ingredients in and just let it simmer away. The more the lentils break down the better it tastes. Make more than you need, then pop it into an old yoghurt pot in the freezer for another day.

a good drizzle of olive oil
4 rashers of smoked streaky bacon, chopped
1 onion, finely chopped
1 stick of celery, finely chopped
1 large carrot, peeled and finely chopped
2 bay leaves
1 large potato, peeled and chopped
200g red lentils
1 sprig of fresh thyme
1 litre chicken or vegetable stock

1. Warm the oil in a large saucepan over a medium heat and fry the bacon until just starting to crisp. Turn down the heat slightly and add the onion, celery, carrot and bay leaves. Season and gently fry, covered, for 10–15 minutes, until softened.

2. Add the chopped potato and fry for a minute or two, then cover the vegetables with the lentils and add the thyme.

3. Pour in the stock, then simmer slowly for 45 minutes–1 hour, stirring every now and then, until the soup is thick and the lentils are soft. Leave to cool slightly before serving with great hunks of bread and cheese.

SERVES	TIME TO PREPARE	TIME TO COOK
2	10 MINUTES	1 HOUR

Chilled watercress and mint soup with pesto

NO FRILLS

Chilled soup – time-forgiving, simple to make, and relaxing to serve – is a blessing to a hurried lifestyle. Serve it straight from the fridge, having made it in advance (up to a week for this one), and pull it out at a moment's notice. Freeze a batch, then let it just defrost – ladle it into guests' glasses pre-dinner as you concentrate on starters and main courses. Pour it into a thermos flask with a few ice cubes and bring it out to slurp mid-walk on a park bench or picnic rug – a rare summer's treat. No reheating unless you want to, no fussing.

There are some soups – most notably herby ones – that taste particularly good cold. Mint keeps its fresh, cooling flavour when iced – warm it up and it can taste quite muddy. Can't find watercress? Use baby leaf spinach and a handful of rocket for pepperiness. Throw finely chopped cucumber into the whizzed pesto for crunch.

a good knob of unsalted butter
1 large onion, finely chopped
1 stick of celery, finely chopped
1 large or 2 small carrots, peeled and finely chopped
2 bay leaves
1 medium potato, peeled and roughly chopped
1.5 litres chicken or vegetable stock
200g watercress, washed, dried and blanched
    in boiling water for a minute, then drained
    and refreshed under cold water (this will help
    keep the colour)
a large handful of fresh mint leaves, chopped

FOR THE PESTO
1 clove of garlic, crushed
2 tablespoons toasted pine nuts
50g Parmesan cheese, grated
a large bunch of basil leaves
a large bunch of mint leaves
50ml extra virgin olive oil
juice of ½ a lemon

SERVES	TIME TO PREPARE	TIME TO COOK
4–6	15 MINUTES	1 HOUR

1. Melt the butter in a large saucepan over a medium-low heat, then add the onion, celery, carrot and bay leaves. Season generously with sea salt and black pepper and gently fry, covered, for 10–15 minutes, until the vegetables are buttery and soft.

2. Add the chopped potato and stir through the vegetables. Pour in the stock and bring to the boil, then gently simmer for 45 minutes, until the vegetables are tender. Set aside to cool slightly.

3. When cooled, add the watercress and mint and blend with a hand whizzer or in a food processor until the soup is completely smooth and bright green. Set aside to cool, then chill in the fridge. Before you serve it, give it a stir.

4. To make the pesto, put the garlic into a mini food processor or a large pestle and mortar with the pine nuts, Parmesan and herbs. Blend to a paste. Slowly pour in the olive oil and whiz or pound until you have a thick pesto. Season with salt and pepper and a squeeze of lemon juice, then loosely stir it through the soup as you serve it.

Spicy lentil and sweet potato soup with lime and coriander

NO FRILLS

This aromatic, spiced soup is an all-year-rounder. It is welcome on a warm evening in the garden, then thaws you through when you're stuck inside, woolly-jumper clad. Garam masala is a blend of warming – not hot – spices that I always have to hand in the kitchen. Just a pinch goes such a long way in curries, and it saves you having to rummage through the spice drawer every time. You can buy decent jars of it – Bart's is good – but making your own is quick and holds buckets of punch. Plump the soup up with prawns, shredded chicken or extra coriander; serve with poppadoms, yoghurt and wedges of lime, and eat bowlfuls of it. Food for the soul.

a knob of unsalted butter
1 onion, finely chopped
1 stick of celery, finely chopped
2 carrots, peeled and finely chopped
3 cloves of garlic, peeled and crushed
a knob of fresh root ginger, peeled and grated
2 teaspoons dried chilli flakes
2 teaspoons garam masala, plus extra to garnish
   (see recipe opposite)
1 sweet potato, peeled and chopped
250g red lentils
1.5 litres chicken or vegetable stock
100ml coconut cream

TO SERVE
thick natural yoghurt, to serve
a squeeze of lime juice
a handful of fresh coriander leaves, chopped
2 fresh red chillies, finely chopped

1. Melt the butter in a large pan over a medium-low heat and gently fry the onion, celery and carrot, covered, for 10–15 minutes, until soft but not coloured. Season generously, then add the garlic and the fresh and dried spices and fry for another 3 minutes.

SERVES	TIME TO PREPARE	TIME TO COOK
4–6	10 MINUTES	1 HOUR

2. Add the the sweet potato and fry for 3 minutes. Pour in the lentils, followed by the stock and the coconut cream, and bring to the boil. Turn down the heat and gently simmer for 45 minutes (the lentils will be tender after 25 minutes, but keep cooking to make more of the flavour).

3. Let the soup cool a little, then, using a hand blender or in a food processor, whiz the soup until smooth. Season well and serve in bowls with a dollop of natural yoghurt, a squeeze of lime, a little pinch of garam masala if you like, a handful of chopped fresh coriander and a scattering of chopped red chilli.

To make your own garam masala

4 tablespoons coriander seeds
1 tablespoon cumin seeds
1 tablespoon black peppercorns
2 teaspoons cumin seeds
2 teaspoons ground ginger or dried galangal
1 teaspoon cardamom seeds (pods discarded – why does no one sell ready-podded cardamom seeds?)
1 teaspoon cloves
a 3cm piece of cinnamon stick
1 bay leaf

Toast the spices, apart from the bay leaf, in a heavy-based frying pan over a medium-low heat until fragrant. Cool slightly, then grind with the bay leaf in a pestle and mortar, coffee grinder or spice grinder. Keep in an airtight jar for up to 3 months.

More ways with garam masala

• Stir into melted butter and toss through cooked rice.
• Whisk it into marinades for lamb or beef on the barbecue.
• Fold it into bread dough.

Onion soup with Gruyère toasts

NIGHT IN

Not the French-style clear onion soup as we know it. This is blended, it's thicker and more hearty, and there is less chance of dropping scalding onions down your chin. Look for large onions with taut skin and a firm body and avoid sprouters. Most bagged-up supermarket onions have almost no flavour when cooked and can leave you with a watery, sorry result. Slice up a few more than you need and freeze them in batches to pull out at other soup-making moments.

a knob of unsalted butter
1kg onions (in good nick), sliced
1 stick of celery, finely chopped
1 clove of garlic, finely chopped
1 potato, peeled and finely chopped
2 bay leaves
1 sprig of fresh thyme
1 sprig of fresh rosemary
750ml fresh chicken or vegetable stock
50ml double cream
2 chunky slices from a white bread loaf
100g Gruyère cheese, grated
chopped fresh parsley leaves, to serve

SERVES	TIME TO PREPARE	TIME TO COOK
2	**20** MINUTES	**1** HOUR

1. Melt the butter in a large saucepan over a medium-low heat and add the onions and celery. Season generously, then gently fry, covered, for 20 minutes, until the onions are soft, gooey and starting to caramelise. Reserve 2 tablespoons of the soft onions for the toasts.

2. Add the garlic and potato and fry briefly, then throw in the herbs and stock. Bring to the boil, then simmer, uncovered, for 40 minutes. Remove from the heat, stir in the cream and allow to cool slightly.

3. Lightly toast the bread, then top it with the reserved onions, season generously and finish with the grated Gruyère. Slide under a hot grill for 3 minutes, until the cheese has melted and is golden and bubbling.

4. Pulse the soup with a hand blender or in a food processor until almost smooth, then season again to taste. Divide into bowls and top with the cheesy toasts and a scattering of chopped parsley.

Celeriac and mustard soup

At the café-cum-bookshop where I used to work, we ate soup with homemade focaccia every day at 11 a.m. before the café filled up. We never got bored with it, even in the heat of summer. Celeriac and mustard soup was a favourite. You could sniff it from way down in the bookshop and out on the street; customers would poke their noses round the door wanting to know what we were having. This is a hailing to that lovely lunch.

Celeriac's knobbly, bulbous outer is in stark contrast to its white, nutty, silken inner but you can still use it – shave off the coarse, gritty bumps, clean them and reserve them for making vegetable stocks.

a knob of unsalted butter

2 large onions, finely chopped

1 large potato, peeled and diced

1kg celeriac, peeled and roughly chopped (keep in a bowl of acidulated water to avoid discoloration)

3 cloves of garlic, peeled and crushed

1.5 litres chicken or vegetable stock

4 tablespoons wholegrain mustard

50ml double cream (optional)

SERVES

4–6

TIME TO PREPARE

15 MINUTES

TIME TO COOK

1 HOUR

1. Melt the butter in a large saucepan over a medium-low heat. Add the onions, season and fry for 10–15 minutes, covered, until softened. Add the potato, celeriac and garlic and fry for another 5 minutes.

2. Pour in the stock, bring to a boil and simmer for 45 minutes, until the celeriac is tender and the stock is flavoursome. Leave to cool slightly, then blitz until smooth. Stir in the mustard and the cream (if using), ladle into large bowls, and swirl through an extra spoonful of cream or crème fraîche.

3 more ways with celeriac

REMOULADE

Mix 500g of peeled and grated raw celeriac with 3 tablespoons of olive oil, 3 tablespoons of crème fraîche, 1 tablespoon of grainy mustard, 3 tablespoons of Dijon mustard, the juice of a lemon and chopped fresh parsley leaves.

MASH

Fry 1kg of peeled and cubed celeriac, a handful of fresh thyme leaves, 2 finely chopped cloves of garlic, and a good pinch of flaked sea salt and freshly ground black pepper in a pan with 2 tablespoons of olive oil over a medium heat for 10 minutes. Add 3–4 tablespoons of stock and simmer for another 10 minutes, until absorbed. Stir in 2 tablespoons of cream and roughly mash.

SALAD

Thinly shave 500g of peeled celeriac and toss with the juice of ½ an orange, 1 teaspoon of Dijon mustard, 1 tablespoon of cider vinegar, a pinch of caster sugar and 4 tablespoons of olive oil. Top with crushed cashew nuts and fresh thyme leaves.

Squash and sage soup

Thoughts of neat pockets of pasta stuffed with pumpkin and drizzled with sage butter have inspired this recipe. Sage leaves are sturdy beings, like sprigs of rosemary and thyme, and can season the squash without changing flavour even under the force of high roasting temperatures. Their earthy aroma and bitter tones go so well with nutty, sweet squash, and are especially delicious crisped up and used as a garnish to this soup. Save the pulp of the squash as you push the soup through a sieve for pasta sauces – just add a little mascarpone or olive oil to loosen it up.

1.2kg firm butternut squash or pumpkin,
    halved, deseeded and quartered
6 cloves of garlic, bashed but not peeled
8 fresh sage leaves
2 tablespoons olive oil,
    plus extra for drizzling
1 red onion, peeled and finely chopped
1 stick of celery, finely chopped
2 carrots, peeled and finely chopped
1 leek, finely chopped
1–2 fresh green chillies, or to taste,
    deseeded and finely chopped
1 bay leaf
a pinch of freshly grated nutmeg
1.5 litres chicken or vegetable stock
mascarpone or crème fraîche, to serve

SERVES	TIME TO PREPARE	TIME TO COOK
4–6	25 MINUTES	1 HOUR

1. Preheat the oven to 200°C/fan 180°C/gas 6. Place the chopped squash, garlic and sage on a baking sheet. Season well, drizzle generously with olive oil, and slide into the oven to roast for 25–30 minutes until golden and tender.

2. Meanwhile, heat 2 tablespoons of oil in a large saucepan over a medium heat and add the onion, celery, carrot and leek. Season, then gently fry, covered, for 10–15 minutes, until softened. Add the chillies, bay leaf and nutmeg and stir. Pour in the stock, bring to the boil and simmer gently for 20 minutes.

3. Remove the squash from the oven and add to the soup, reserving half the crisped sage leaves. Squeeze the garlic cloves out of their skins and stir into the soup. Simmer for another 5–10 minutes, then allow to cool slightly and blend in a food processor or with a hand blender. Season to taste. Stir in a dollop of savoury mascarpone or tangy crème fraîche, and top with the reserved sage leaves to serve.

Indian-spiced cauliflower soup

Take the curry base to this soup and mix it up with any vegetable you like. Bold, wintry roots like squash and parsnip work particularly nicely. Sweet, nutty cauliflower is a great brassica to blend, turning creamy as soon as you whiz it. Fresh curry leaves have a distinct nutty smell which kicks off the spices – they crop up in most Asian supermarkets and you can buy them online. It's worth having a rootle round for a large bunch – you can freeze any that you don't use. If you can't find them, a pinch of mild curry powder is a good replacement. Don't forget the mango raita – it relaxes the heat of the spices and hits you with little sweet surprises.

1 teaspoon brown mustard seeds, plus extra to serve
1 teaspoon cumin seeds
1 teaspoon coriander seeds
1½ teaspoons ground turmeric
1 tablespoon vegetable oil
1 onion, grated
1 medium-hot red chilli, sliced
1 stick of celery, grated
2 cloves of garlic, finely sliced
a 6cm piece of fresh root ginger, peeled and grated
1 potato, peeled and roughly chopped
1 large head of cauliflower, leaves removed, broken
    into smaller florets
1.5 litres chicken stock
1 handful of fresh curry leaves

FOR THE MANGO RAITA
100g Greek yoghurt
1 ripe mango, peeled and chopped
¼ of a cucumber, peeled and chopped
a handful of fresh mint leaves, finely chopped
½ teaspoon flaked sea salt

SERVES	TIME TO PREPARE	TIME TO COOK
6 IN DEEP BOWLS	**20** MINUTES	**1** HOUR **10** MINUTES

1. Heat a pan over a medium-low heat and add the mustard, cumin and coriander seeds. Dry fry for 5 minutes until fragrant and the mustard seeds start to pop (take care not to burn them), then add the turmeric. Remove from the pan and grind to a fine powder in a pestle and mortar or spice grinder.

2. Heat the oil in a large saucepan over a medium heat and add the onion, chilli, celery, garlic and ginger. Season well with salt and pepper and gently fry, covered, for 10–15 minutes, until soft. Add the potato, the cauliflower and the spice blend and fry for another 5 minutes. Pour in the stock, add the curry leaves, bring to the boil and simmer for 45 minutes, until the vegetables are tender. Cool slightly, then whiz in a food processor or with a hand blender until smooth.

3. To make the raita, mix the yoghurt with the mango and cucumber and season well with salt and pepper. Dollop into the soup, and sprinkle over a few brown mustard seeds to serve.

Clam chowder

Chowder – such a pleasing name – waves to north Aberdeenshire with its famous smoked haddock Cullen Skink, or to east coast America where they blend crumbly saltines into their clam soup. Combining starchy potato, lots of cream, and salty bacon is no skinny meal, but it is such a joy to eat. When you steam open the clams in wine, they produce the most delicious stock to pour into the soup. The tasty little clams are added without shell, balancing the velvety textures and the saltiness of the soup with their succulent meat. Check that the clam shells are unbroken and that the clams are still alive; tap the shells gently on the tabletop – if they close slowly, they're alive. Discard any that stay open. Rinse the clams in running clean, cold water to remove the grit.

1kg small clams
200ml cider or white wine
a good knob of unsalted butter
50g thickly sliced smoked bacon, cut into small dice
2 leeks, finely sliced
1 stick of celery, finely chopped
1 bay leaf
2 large potatoes, peeled and diced
300ml whole milk
120ml double cream
2 tablespoons chopped fresh parsley leaves
2 tablespoons chopped fresh tarragon

SERVES

4

TIME TO PREPARE

20 MINS + CLEANING THE CLAMS

TIME TO COOK

40 MINUTES

1. Put a large pan over a high heat and add the small, cleaned clams and cider or white wine. Bring the boil, then cover and boil for 5 minutes, until the clams are all open, discarding any that are still closed. Remove from the heat and drain, reserving the cooking juices.

2. Heat the butter in the same pan over a medium-low heat and add the smoked bacon, frying for 5 minutes until starting to crisp. Add the leeks, celery and bay leaf and sweat gently, covered, for 10 minutes. Pour in a few tablespoons of the clam juices.

3. Drop the chopped potatoes into a pan of lightly salted water and bring to the boil. Simmer for 7–10 minutes, or until tender. Drain and add to the leeks.

4. Stir in the milk and cream, then turn the heat to low and simmer to reduce by a quarter. Remove the meat from the clams and add to the pot. Stir in the herbs and ladle into shallow bowls. Serve with crusty bread, or top with broken crackers.

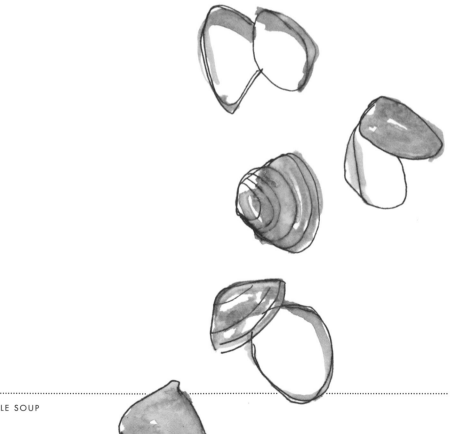

Crab bisque

The sea-flavoured crab shells, the rusty brown meat and a splosh of sweet brandy turn this humble soup into a bisque for kings. Don't go overboard on serving sizes – there's no denying this is a very rich soup. In fact, a few mouthfuls each is enough. Fill small bowls to go round, or even little sherry glasses to slurp from for a pre-dinner whetter. Stir in leftovers to thin out sauces for crab tarts or gratins, or freeze spoonfuls in ice cube trays to add more power to fish stocks and other soups.

If you ever eat crab, lobster or shell-on prawns, keep the shells – use them, crushed, to flavour this soup. Find cooked crab in their shells at a trusted fishmonger's. If buying a crab to cook, always buy it live and then dispatch it, or ask the fishmonger to do it for you – you don't know how long the dead, raw ones have been sitting there.

1 tablespoon olive oil
2 small onions, finely chopped
1 leek, sliced
2 carrots, peeled and finely chopped
1 stick of celery, finely chopped
3 cloves of garlic, sliced
2 bay leaves
1 tablespoon fennel seeds
1 picked, cooked crab shell, claws and all, roughly crushed inside a large ziplock bag with a rolling pin
1 tablespoon tomato purée
a splash of brandy
2 teaspoons cayenne pepper, plus extra to serve
1 x 400g tin of chopped tomatoes
500ml fresh fish stock
50ml double cream
150–200g mix of brown and white crabmeat
chopped fresh tarragon, to serve

SERVES

10 AS A STARTER

TIME TO PREPARE

25 MINUTES

TIME TO COOK

1 HOUR **15** MINUTES

1. Heat the olive oil in a large heavy-based saucepan, then add the onion, leek, carrot, celery, garlic, bay leaves and fennel seeds. Season generously and gently fry, covered, for 10 minutes, until the vegetables have softened. Add the crab shells. Stir in the tomato purée, brandy and cayenne, then turn up the heat and simmer for 5 minutes, until the alcohol has evaporated. Pour in the chopped tomatoes and the fish stock, bring to the boil, then reduce the heat and simmer for 45 minutes, until the stock is well flavoured. Allow to cool slightly.

2. Transfer the soup to a food processor and pulse briefly. Strain the soup, shells and all, through a fine sieve lined with an unloved tea towel or a sheet of muslin over a large jug, pressing the bits with a wooden spoon or a silicone scraper so that the juices seep into the liquid. Discard the debris.

3. Return the strained soup to a clean pan and stir in the cream. Simmer for another 5 minutes, then stir through the white and brown crabmeat. Season to taste, and serve with an extra sprinkling of cayenne and chopped tarragon.

Pair simple, mild ingredients to eat crab at its best:

Crab, chilli, lemon and parsley spaghetti: Cook the spaghetti until *al dente*, then drain. Mix crabmeat with finely chopped red chilli, lemon zest and juice to taste and lots of finely chopped fresh parsley. Add crème fraîche, if you like. Stir the crab into the pasta, season and serve.

Crab omelette: Whisk eggs, finely chopped chives and brown crabmeat in a bowl. Season. Heat butter in a non-stick frying pan. Pour in the egg mixture and scramble the eggs briefly with a spatula, then leave to almost set. Add white crabmeat, fold omelette over the filling, and serve.

Crab salad with lime, avocado, chilli and coriander: Toss white crabmeat with roughly chopped avocado, finely chopped red chilli, lime juice and fresh coriander leaves.

Crab, yoghurt and cayenne on toast: In a small bowl, mix together white and brown crabmeat with enough yoghurt to make a loose pâté. Season well with salt and pepper and a good pinch of cayenne for a kick. Serve on warm brown toasts, with lemon wedges on the side.

Crab gratin (see page 196)

Fresh garlic vichyssoise

Fresh garlic – also known as wet garlic or new season garlic – has a short picking life, between early May and mid June, before it is hung up to dry. The skins are unformed, the cloves are soft and the pale green stems are easy to slice, assuming the delicate texture of young leeks. They are forgivingly mild, and are often eaten raw, so cooking with a large amount won't make you the enemy of the household. If you want more punch, wild garlic shares the same season and has a stronger effect, so blanch it quickly and stir it into the soup before serving. Don't worry if you can't find either of these – use young garlic cloves that aren't sprouting green stalks (remove the inner green stem if necessary, as this can be bitter and cause indigestion). Vichyssoise? A glorified title for leek and potato soup.

You can make this up to 2 days in advance – add the cream at the last minute to avoid the soup splitting. Have this hot, too, if you like.

a knob of unsalted butter

1 large onion, finely chopped

1–2 leeks, thoroughly rinsed, roughly chopped, white bit only (400g)

15 cloves of fresh garlic, peeled and sliced (see introduction), or 6 large young cloves of garlic

1 potato, peeled and chopped

1.5 litres chicken or vegetable stock

150ml double cream

¼ teaspoon ground mace or freshly grated nutmeg

¼ teaspoon flaked sea salt, plus extra to serve

a generous pinch of coarsely ground black pepper

2 ice cubes

4–6 quail's eggs

olive oil, for drizzling

1. Melt the butter in a medium pan. Add the onion, leeks and garlic, season generously, and slowly cook, covered, for 10–15 minutes, to soften but not colour.

2. Add the potato and fry for 5 minutes before pouring in the stock. Increase the heat and bring to the boil, then simmer gently for 45 minutes until the potato is tender.

3. Leave the soup to cool slightly, then add the cream, season well to taste, add the ground mace or grated nutmeg, and whiz in a liquidiser or with a hand blender. Push through a sieve into a jug, discarding any chunky debris, and taste again for seasoning.

4. Cool the soup completely, then add the ice cubes, cover and leave in the fridge until ready to serve. Stir through at the last minute.

5. Just before serving, bring a small pan of water to the boil. Take the pan off the heat. Carefully crack in the quail's eggs, one by one, from a small cup that is almost touching the surface of the water. Leave to poach for 1 minute, until the white is firm and the yolk is soft, then remove with a slotted spoon and put into a bowl of ice cold water. Pour the soup into bowls and serve each with a poached quail's egg, a drizzle of olive oil and a pinch of flaked sea salt.

SERVES

4–6

TIME TO PREPARE

15 MINUTES

TIME TO COOK

1 HOUR

Healing chicken soup

QUICK FIX

A surefire way to fix a grump. The secret to this clear, spicy, health-boosting broth is the garnish – serve the soup alongside bowls of fresh herbs and hot red chilli, to add as you slurp.

200g egg noodles
olive oil, for greasing
a knob of unsalted butter
1 large red onion, finely sliced
2 sticks of celery, finely sliced lengthways
1 large or 2 small carrots, peeled and shredded
2 bay leaves
1 sprig of fresh thyme, leaves picked
1 litre fresh chicken stock
4 free-range skinless, boneless chicken thighs, sliced

TO SERVE
a large bunch of fresh parsley, chopped
a large bunch of fresh tarragon, chopped
a small bunch of fresh mint leaves, chopped
2 soft-boiled eggs (6 minutes from boiling), halved
1–2 red chillies, sliced

SERVES

4

TIME TO PREPARE

15 MINUTES

TIME TO COOK

1 HOUR 15 MINUTES

1. Bring a pan of water to the boil and add the noodles. Cook for 15 minutes, or according to the packet instructions. Drain and refresh under cold water, then toss with a little olive oil to stop them sticking together. Set aside until needed.

2. Melt the butter in the same pan over a medium-low heat, then add the onion, celery, carrot and herbs. Season generously with sea salt and black pepper, then gently fry, covered, for 10–15 minutes, until the vegetables are buttery and soft.

3. Pour in the stock. Cover and bring to the boil, then turn down the heat to a gentle simmer. Add the chicken and simmer, covered, for roughly 45 minutes, until the vegetables and chicken are tender.

4. Divide the cooked noodles between 4 bowls and ladle over the soup. Serve with the chopped parsley, tarragon and mint, half an egg each and a sprinkling of sliced red chilli.

Beans and greens broth

This is a brilliant way to jazz up an old soup and make it last longer. The addition of leftover soup, whatever it is, acts like a stock cube, boosting the flavour of the stock you add. Blanch the cabbage to keep it bright and tender, then stir in the lettuce for more crunch.

a knob of unsalted butter

1 onion, finely sliced

1 stick of celery, finely sliced

1 small leek, finely sliced

2 cloves of garlic, finely sliced

¼ teaspoon dried chilli flakes

1 bay leaf

500ml leftover soup (see introduction)

1.5 litres chicken or vegetable stock

500g white cabbage or pointed cabbage,
    finely sliced

1 x 400g tin of cannellini or haricot beans, rinsed

100g round lettuce, roughly sliced

a small handful of chopped fresh tarragon

Parmesan cheese, shaved, to serve (optional)

SERVES	TIME TO PREPARE	TIME TO COOK
4	15 MINUTES	50 MINUTES

1. Melt the butter in a large saucepan over a medium heat and add the onion, celery, leek and garlic. Season, then gently fry, covered, for 10–15 minutes, until softened. Add the chilli flakes and bay leaf, season and stir. Pour in the leftover soup and the stock (or if making fresh, just add the stock), then bring to the boil and simmer for 30 minutes.

2. Add the cabbage and beans and simmer for another 3 minutes, until the cabbage is tender and the beans are soft and warmed through. Stir in the lettuce and let it wilt, then sprinkle with chopped tarragon and serve immediately, with torn bread and shavings of Parmesan, if you like it.

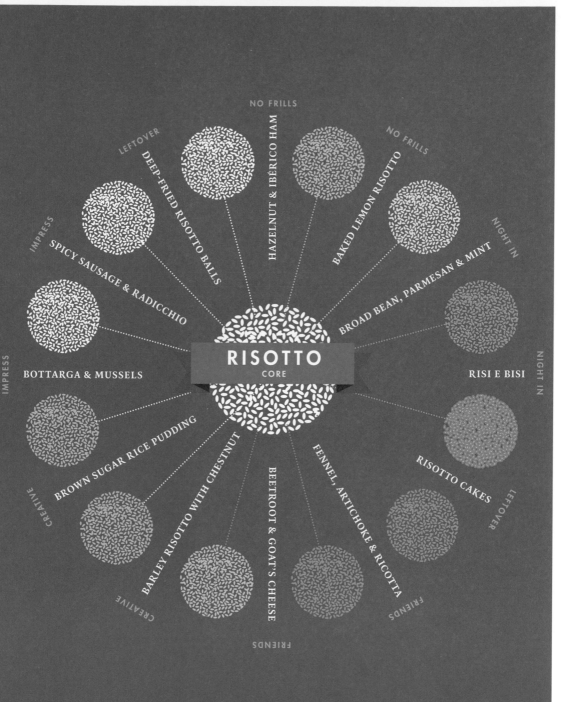

NO FRILLS

NO FRILLS

LEFTOVER

DEEP-FRIED RISOTTO BALLS

HAZELNUT & IBÉRICO HAM

BAKED LEMON RISOTTO

IMPRESS

SPICY SAUSAGE & RADICCHIO

NIGHT IN

BROAD BEAN, PARMESAN & MINT

IMPRESS

BOTTARGA & MUSSELS

RISOTTO
CORE

NIGHT IN

RISI E BISI

BROWN SUGAR RICE PUDDING

RISOTTO CAKES

CREATIVE

BARLEY RISOTTO WITH CHESTNUT

BEETROOT & GOAT'S CHEESE

FENNEL, ARTICHOKE & RICOTTA

LEFTOVER

CREATIVE

FRIENDS

FRIENDS

Risotto

There's nothing much more homely and comforting than a buttery risotto, eaten from a bowl with a spoon. Risotto is one recipe to have permanently lodged in your brain – if you've cooked it once you'll know how long it takes to prepare, what you want to look for in the rice, how much seasoning you like, and that a lot of Parmesan is key. No faff, and easy to do.

Its mild-tasting base is a great platform for experimentation. There is nothing that you can't fold into a white risotto – just consider the flavours that work together first, or what you've got left in the fridge, and go from there. When you use good-quality ingredients – especially well-made stock – you'll notice a significant improvement in flavour, but the most brilliant thing about risotto is it can zest up old ingredients and make them taste wonderfully fresh. Next time, try a different rice – arborio, carnaroli, vialone nano – add chilli to the onions, use up that leftover courgette, or stir in the bottarga you've been patiently waiting to cook with. Here are a few recipes that will nudge you in the right direction.

Risotto know-how

- You can use any short-grain rice for a risotto, but arborio is the most widely available. It absorbs the stock well, holds its oval shape and makes a delicious smooth and silky sauce – too much cooking can make it stodgy, though. Carnaroli and vialone nano are less easy to get hold of and more expensive, but are more suited to lighter, looser risottos. They have a higher starch level than arborio, giving a more creamy risotto, and a slightly larger grain, making it more likely to withstand overcooking.

- Make sure you cook off the wine well or it can make your risotto sharp.

- You want your risotto to ooze, to slide on the plate – not to be claggy and stiff. Toasting the rice well, the addition of butter before resting, and perhaps a little more stock than the rice needs will give you a juicy bowl, loose enough to need the help of a spoon to eat it.

- Risotto is best served immediately, so there is not much scope for making it all in advance. You can, however, stop a risotto after you've added the wine and leave it to cool. Keep it covered like this in the fridge for up to 3 days before finishing the recipe. If you want a less hands-on risotto than the usual, make the base, then throw in the stock and bake it (see baked lemon risotto, page 70).

White risotto

Making a good risotto is really not as laborious as most people think. Half an hour of gentle stirring and cooking – while chatting, dancing, drinking, building up an appetite – and it's ready. The trick is finely chopped vegetables, very good stock – you can buy lovely fresh stocks which tend to be purer and less herby than stock pots and cubes, and if you've got homemade even better (see chicken stock, page 110) – freshly grated nutmeg to cut through the creaminess, and plenty of Parmesan. This core recipe is an easy starting point for making delicious risotto – from here you can add, remove, bake, fry, and, using almost exactly the same technique, make something sweet.

2 tablespoons extra virgin olive oil, plus extra
    for drizzling (optional)
50g unsalted butter
1 onion, very finely chopped
1 stick of celery, very finely chopped
a pinch of freshly grated nutmeg
2 cloves of garlic, finely chopped
250g risotto rice
175ml white wine or vermouth
750ml–1 litre fresh chicken or vegetable stock,
    kept warm over a low heat
100g Parmesan cheese, grated

SERVES

4

TIME TO PREPARE

10 MINUTES

TIME TO COOK

30 MINUTES

1. Heat the olive oil and half the butter in a large saucepan over a medium-low heat and add the onion, celery and nutmeg – the spice will impart its piney, peppery flavour to the onion and strengthen the base of the dish early on. Season, then cover and gently cook for 10 minutes, until the onions are soft but uncoloured, and have almost lost their shape. Stir in the garlic and fry for a further 1 minute, being careful not to burn it.

2. Add the risotto rice and fry for 3 minutes or so, until almost translucent. Turn up the heat and add the wine, simmering for 2 minutes, until most of the alcohol has evaporated and the liquid is absorbed. (You can stop cooking a risotto at this stage and, when cooled, keep it in the fridge covered for up to 3 days before finishing the recipe.)

3. Pour over a little stock and stir until the rice has absorbed all the liquid – you should be able to see the bottom of the pan as you stir. Repeat this process, adding a little splash of stock at a time, until the rice is just soft – it should be a little over *al dente*. This should take about 20 minutes. Use more stock or water and stir for a little longer if the rice needs more cooking.

4. Once cooked, stir in the remaining butter and the Parmesan. Take the rice off the heat and leave it to sit, covered, for a minute or two so the cheese and butter can melt into the risotto and the rice can relax. Season again, and serve immediately in shallow bowls, drizzling over more olive oil if you like.

White risotto with sherry, Ibérico ham and hazelnut dressing

NO FRILLS

Sweetening, syrupy booze is an essential part of making risotto. Burning off the alcohol, with the rice turning pale in the pan, leaves behind a sumptuous combination of sharpness and sugar, and helps to intensify everything else you put in the dish. Match the grog to the other ingredients you want to use. Here I've injected Spain into Italy, with nuts, cured ham and rosemary, so this time it's having a good slog of sticky, fortified sherry. Sweet Pedro Ximénez is bottle of choice for its likeness to treacle – very sweet but balanced by the salty ham, Grana Padano and creamy hazelnuts. One for the risotto, one for the cook …

1 tablespoon olive oil

25g butter

2 shallots, very finely chopped, and 10 shallots, peeled and left whole

leaves from a sprig of fresh rosemary, plus extra to serve

250g risotto rice

100ml sweet Pedro Ximénez or oloroso sherry

1 litre good-quality chicken stock, heated

50g Manchego (a salty, nutty Spanish cheese which works well in place of Parmesan)

75g sliced Ibérico ham

chopped fresh parsley leaves, to serve

FOR THE DRESSING (OPTIONAL)

100g hazelnuts, chopped and toasted

1 small clove of garlic

½ teaspoon flaked sea salt

2 teaspoons sherry vinegar

100ml extra virgin olive oil

lemon juice, to taste

SERVES	TIME TO PREPARE	TIME TO COOK
4	10 MINUTES	30 MINUTES

1. First make the hazelnut dressing (if using). Place the hazelnuts, garlic, salt and vinegar in a food processor and whiz to fine paste. Slowly pour in the olive oil, still whizzing, until it begins to emulsify. Season to taste, perhaps with a little lemon juice if you like, and set aside.

2. Heat the olive oil and half of the butter in a large pan. Add the chopped and whole shallots – some are left whole for more texture – then season and stir in the rosemary leaves. Fry, covered, for 15 minutes, until buttery and beginning to caramelise. Remove half the whole shallots from the pan and set aside.

3. Stir the rice into the buttery shallots that are left in the pan and fry for 10 minutes, stirring until translucent. Pour in the sherry and turn up the heat. Bubble for 3 minutes, stirring until the rice has absorbed all the liquid. (Pause the recipe here if needed.) Little by little, pour in the stock, adding more as it gets absorbed, stirring after each addition. Repeat this until you have no more stock and the rice is tender, buttery and sweet. Stir in the remaining butter and the Manchego, then take off the heat and leave it to sit, covered, for a minute or two. Serve in shallow bowls and top with the reserved shallots, a few rosemary leaves and the slices of Ibérico ham, and drizzle on the hazelnut dressing (if using). Sprinkle with chopped parsley.

Baked lemon risotto

NO FRILLS

Oven-baked risotto requires almost no stirring – it's the perfect option for nights when you'd rather relax than be in the kitchen. Once the base of the risotto has been fried with the rice and wine, all the stock goes in at once and it is transferred to the oven to continue cooking. Before you know it, you're left with a golden crust and perfectly cooked rice. This risotto has a wonderful cleanness – lemon zest and juice cut through the creamy butter, and rosemary lends a little smokiness – and it is so easy to make. Serve as a side dish to grilled fish or on its own for a light main course.

50g unsalted butter
2 tablespoons extra virgin olive oil
4 shallots, very finely chopped
1 stick of celery, very finely chopped
2 cloves of garlic, finely chopped
a pinch of freshly grated nutmeg
300g risotto rice
175ml white wine or vermouth
juice of 2 lemons and finely grated zest of 1 lemon
750ml chicken or vegetable stock, heated
a sprig of fresh rosemary, plus extra to garnish
100g Parmesan cheese, grated

SERVES	SERVES	TIME TO PREPARE	TIME TO COOK
4–6 AS A MAIN	10 AS A SIDE	10 MINUTES	40 MINUTES

1. Preheat the oven to 150°C/fan 130°C/gas 1. Melt half the butter with the olive oil in an ovenproof frying pan over a medium-low heat. Add the shallots and celery, season, then fry, covered, for 10 minutes until soft. Add the garlic and nutmeg and fry for another minute or two before stirring in the rice. Coat the rice in the buttery vegetables and fry for about 5 minutes, until almost translucent.

2. Pour over the wine and turn up the heat. Let the wine bubble for a few minutes until it has evaporated and been absorbed by the rice. (Pause the recipe here if needed.) Stir in the lemon juice and zest and season well. Add the stock to the pan with the rosemary, then cover with a lid or foil and transfer to the oven – alternatively you can move the risotto to a warmed ovenproof dish, and cover with foil. Bake for 15–20 minutes, until the rice is just tender.

3. Take the pan from the oven, remove the lid or foil and grate the Parmesan on top of the risotto. Turn the oven setting to a medium grill and slide the pan or dish underneath, uncovered. Grill for 5–10 minutes, until golden and bubbling. Season again, and serve with an extra rosemary sprig.

Broad bean, Parmesan and mint risotto

NIGHT IN

I'd eat this every day, especially when broad beans are available fresh in their pods from May to September. Sweet, buttery broads love pork, so adding crispy, salty pancetta rounds up all the flavours of the risotto and makes for the most delicious forkful. A little bit of mint will go a long way – take it to the table in a separate bowl, to stir in as you go.

200g freshly podded or frozen broad beans
1 tablespoon extra virgin olive oil, plus an extra
   teaspoon for the pancetta and for drizzling
25g unsalted butter
1 small onion, finely chopped
1 stick of celery, finely chopped
a pinch of freshly grated nutmeg
2 cloves of garlic, crushed
150g risotto rice
175ml white wine or vermouth
600ml fresh chicken or vegetable stock, heated
50g smoked pancetta, cubed
50g Parmesan cheese, grated
a small handful of fresh mint leaves, finely sliced
pea shoots, to serve

SERVES

2

TIME TO PREPARE

20 MINUTES

TIME TO COOK

25 MINUTES

1. Bring a pan of water to the boil and add the broad beans. After 2 minutes, drain and refresh under cold water. Pop the bright green beans out of their skins into another bowl of cold water and set aside (younger beans may not need popping, but the skins can often be bitter and rubbery).

2. Heat the olive oil and half the butter in a large saucepan over a medium-low heat and add the onion, celery and nutmeg. Season and gently fry for 10 minutes, covered, until the onions are very soft and have almost lost their shape. Add the garlic and stir through, frying for a further minute.

3. Add the risotto rice and fry for 5 minutes or so, until almost translucent. Turn up the heat and add the wine, simmering for a few minutes until the alcohol has evaporated and the liquid is absorbed. (Pause the recipe here if needed.)

4. Add the stock a little at a time as the rice absorbs it. Continue, stirring, until you have finished all the stock and the rice is tender.

5. Meanwhile, heat a little oil in a pan over a medium heat and fry the pancetta until crisp and golden. Set aside. Add the remaining butter to the risotto with the Parmesan and a generous pinch of salt and pepper and rest. Stir in the cooked and podded broad beans with the mint. Top with the crispy pancetta and pea shoots, drizzle with olive oil and serve.

Risi e bisi

What a stroke of Venetian genius to make an already simple risotto even less work. The result is soupy, slurpable, and is probably one of the most soothing dishes to eat. Sometimes, when all I want is minimal effort and maximum end, I leave the risotto to very slowly simmer with all the stock, and let it cook itself, scraping the bottom of the pan once in a while. Add crispy pancetta if you're in need of more salt.

1 tablespoon olive oil

10g butter

2 banana shallots, very finely chopped

white part of a small leek, finely sliced

125g risotto rice

175ml white wine or vermouth

600ml excellent-quality fresh chicken stock, heated

200g freshly podded or frozen peas, defrosted

75g Grana Padano cheese, finely grated

a small handful of fresh parsley, chopped, to serve

1. Melt the oil with 5g of the butter in a pan and add the shallots and leek. Season, then fry, covered, for 10 minutes, until softened. Add the risotto rice and fry for 5 minutes, stirring, until almost translucent, then turn up the heat, add the wine and bubble until absorbed. (Pause the recipe here if needed.)

2. Season well, then gradually add the stock, a ladleful at a time, stirring after each addition until the liquid has been fully absorbed before adding the next ladleful. Once the rice is cooked you should have a soupy-looking risotto. Stir in the peas with the grated Grana Padano, the remaining butter and parsley. Take the rice off the heat and leave it to sit, covered, for a minute or two, then serve.

SERVES	TIME TO PREPARE	TIME TO COOK
2	10 MINUTES	30 MINUTES

Risotto cakes

LEFTOVER LOVE

For those moments when you pour in too much risotto rice and have bowls of the stuff left. Oh so simple. Serve with fried eggs and salad, or smoked salmon.

200g cold leftover risotto
1 large free-range egg, beaten
25g plain flour
a knob of butter or a drizzle of olive oil

1. Mix the leftover risotto with the beaten egg, then season and mould into 4 x 50g balls. Dust with a little flour, flatten gently into patties, and set aside on a lined baking sheet.

2. Melt the butter or oil in a wide frying pan and, when bubbling, add the cakes. Fry for 4 minutes on each side, until crisp, and serve for breakfast with eggs and smoked salmon.

MAKES

4 CAKES

READY IN

15 MINUTES

Fennel, artichoke and ricotta risotto

FEEDING FRIENDS

If I can get my hands on a perky, purple baby artichoke, I go to the necessary lengths to cook up fresh hearts just for this. Trim the stalk and tip and pull off any tough outer leaves, then boil the whole choke in boiling salted water with a few lemon slices and 2 whole garlic cloves for 20 minutes. Drain, then tug to remove the tender leaves until you get to the fibrous centre. Scrape the fibres away and there you'll find the heart. Chop up and add to the risotto. Keep the leaves and scrape up the flesh with your teeth as you cook. Otherwise jarred hearts will most definitely do. Crumble in ricotta and cooked fennel with the artichokes for extra creaminess. It's a mild tasting risotto, light and summery, with some of my favourite vegetables – serve it up on a platter with plenty of extra olive oil, sea salt and grated Parmesan on the table.

2 tablespoons extra virgin olive oil
50g unsalted butter
1 onion, finely chopped
1 stick of celery, finely chopped
1 large fennel bulb, finely sliced or shaved
    with a mandoline
1 tablespoon fennel seeds
a pinch of freshly grated nutmeg
2 cloves of garlic, finely chopped
250g risotto rice
175ml white wine or vermouth
750ml–1 litre fresh chicken or vegetable stock, heated
4 fresh, cooked artichoke hearts (see introduction),
    finely sliced, or 100g artichoke hearts in oil,
    drained and finely sliced
grated zest of ½ a lemon
150g Parmesan cheese, grated
100g ricotta cheese

SERVES	TIME TO PREPARE	TIME TO COOK
4–6	10 MINUTES	30 MINUTES

1. Heat the olive oil and half the butter in a large saucepan over a medium-low heat and add the onion, celery, fennel, fennel seeds and nutmeg. Season and gently fry for 10 minutes, covered, until the onions are very soft but uncoloured and have almost lost their shape. Add the garlic and stir through, frying for 1 minute.

2. Add the risotto rice and fry for 5 minutes or so until almost translucent. Turn up the heat and add the wine or vermouth, simmering for a few minutes until the alcohol has evaporated and the liquid is absorbed. (Pause the recipe here if needed.)

3. Pour over a little stock and stir until the rice has absorbed all the liquid. You should be able to see the bottom of the pan here. Repeat this process, adding a little splash of stock at a time, stirring, until the rice is soft. The rice should be a little over *al dente*. Use more stock or water if the rice needs more cooking.

4. When the rice is almost cooked, add the finely sliced fresh artichoke or the drained hearts and stir through to warm. Stir in the remaining butter, the lemon zest, Parmesan and ricotta and season well. Take the rice off the heat and leave it to sit, covered, for a minute or two, then serve immediately in shallow bowls.

Beetroot and goat's cheese risotto

What is needed here is an excellent bunch of purple beetroot, rubber gloves and a good grater. This is fun. I grate the beetroot in raw to keep the deep crimson colour and the clean, nutty flavours that are so prominent and earthy in uncooked beets. It's not all soil and grass, though. Adding a hearty spoonful of sharp soft goat's cheese loosens up the rice, making it creamy, and gives it a kick of umami. If in doubt about what to pair with 'troots, cheese in any form and flavour makes a loyal companion.

If you'd prefer your beetroots cooked, preheat the oven to 200°C/fan 180°C/gas 6. Wrap the beetroots in foil and roast on a baking tray in the oven for 40–45 minutes, until tender all the way through. Remove and set aside to cool. Alternatively, poach them in a pan of salted boiling water for 40 minutes. When the beetroot is cool enough to handle, peel back the skin with your thumb and coarsely grate them. (You may want to wear plastic gloves for this.)

2 tablespoons extra virgin olive oil
25g unsalted butter
1 onion, finely chopped
1 stick of celery, finely chopped
a pinch of freshly grated nutmeg
2 cloves of garlic, finely chopped
250g risotto rice
175ml white wine or vermouth
750ml–1 litre fresh chicken or vegetable stock, heated
4 large beetroots, scrubbed, topped and tailed, then peeled and grated (stems blanched and reserved (optional))
50g soft goat's cheese
fresh thyme leaves, to serve

SERVES

4–6

TIME TO PREPARE

20 MINUTES

TIME TO COOK

30 MINUTES

1. Heat the olive oil and half the butter in a large saucepan over a medium-low heat and add the onion, celery and nutmeg. Season and gently fry for 10 minutes, covered, until the onions are very soft and have almost lost their shape. Add the garlic and stir through, frying for 1 minute.

2. Add the risotto rice and fry for 5 minutes or so until almost translucent. Turn up the heat and add the wine, simmering for a few minutes until the alcohol has evaporated and the liquid is absorbed. (Pause the recipe here if needed.)

3. Pour over a little stock and stir until the rice has absorbed all the liquid. You should be able to see the bottom of the pan here. Repeat this process, adding a little splash of stock at a time, stirring, until the rice is soft. The rice should be a little over *al dente*. Use more stock or water if the rice needs more cooking.

4. When the rice is cooked, stir in the grated beetroot with the remaining butter and 40g of the goat's cheese. You will get a vibrant purple colour.

5. Take the rice off the heat and serve in shallow bowls, topped with the blanched beetroot stems (if using), the remaining goat's cheese and a few fresh thyme leaves.

3 more ways with beetroot

ROAST BEET SALAD

Roast the beetroots and chop. Place in a roasting tin with chunkily chopped sweet potatoes and roast again for 20 minutes. Toss with olive oil, oregano, walnuts and halloumi.

BEETROOT CARPACCIO

Very thinly slice raw, peeled beetroot and toss with a dressing made with 1 teaspoon of sherry vinegar, ½ teaspoon of Dijon mustard, a squeeze of dark honey, a pinch of salt and 3 teaspoons of olive oil.

PICKLED BEETS

Slice cooked beetroots. Simmer equal measures of sugar and cider vinegar for 15 minutes. Add sliced, cooked beetroot and fresh tarragon leaves, then pack into a sterilised jar with a tightly fitting lid. Store for up to 3 months and eat with a pork pie.

Creamy barley risotto with chestnuts, porcini and cavolo nero

GET CREATIVE

Not that a risotto ever gets same-old, but on occasion it's great to try new ways and new textures. Barley grains have a wonderfully waxy chew; mushrooms and chestnuts melt as you close your teeth on them; and cavolo nero throws in a bit of crunch. This rounded risotto has plenty of character and substance but if you want an even creamier version, stir in nutty blue cheese.

500g cavolo nero leaves, thick stalks trimmed

50g unsalted butter

2 tablespoons extra virgin olive oil

1 onion, very finely chopped

1 stick of celery, very finely chopped

a pinch of freshly grated nutmeg

3 cloves of garlic, finely chopped

100g ready-cooked chestnuts, half crushed, half finely chopped

30g dried porcini mushrooms, rehydrated in just-boiled water for 20 minutes

250g pearl barley (you can swap this for risotto rice if you like)

175ml white wine or vermouth

750ml–1 litre fresh chicken or vegetable stock, heated

20g pecorino cheese, grated, plus extra to serve (a hard sheep's cheese – delicious with porcini)

2 tablespoons double cream

SERVES	TIME TO PREPARE	TIME TO COOK
4–6	15 MINUTES	25 MINUTES

1. Bring a large pan of lightly salted water to the boil. When boiling, lower in the cavolo nero and cook on a simmer for 2–3 minutes, until bright green and tender. Drain and refresh under ice-cold water to keep it fresh. When cool enough, squeeze out any excess water, then set aside.

2. Melt the butter with the oil in a pan and add the onion and celery. Season and fry for 10 minutes, covered, until softened and almost caramelised. Stir in the nutmeg, garlic, crushed chestnuts and drained rehydrated mushrooms. Sprinkle in the pearl barley and fry for 2 minutes, stirring. Pour in the wine and bubble for a few minutes until absorbed. (Pause the recipe here if needed.)

3. Gradually add the hot stock (including the mushroom soaking liquid – strained of any grit – if you like), a ladleful at a time, stirring after each addition until the liquid has been fully absorbed before adding the next ladleful. When the barley is tender, stir in the cavolo nero to warm through.

4. Just before you serve, add the rest of the butter, the pecorino and the cream. Take the risotto off the heat, and leave to stand, covered, for 5 minutes. Serve in shallow bowls and top with the chopped chestnuts and a sprinkling of sea salt and black pepper.

Brown sugar rice pudding

GET CREATIVE

OK, so not a risotto, but we're not far off. Risotto rice is a hero for sweet things too. It goes into the oven just like a baked risotto but at a lower heat and for a longer time, so it really gets a chance to ooze and crisp.

This is a perfect opportunity to play with flavour. For a more luxurious and celebratory version, try pouring in Amaretto, Marsala or molasses-like oloroso sherry before you add the sugar; grate in orange or lemon zest or stud it with pieces of chocolate; bake it in individual dishes at the same temperature for almost an hour, checking for your preferred consistency. The rice will be cooked about 30 minutes into the baking; the rest of the time it will be soaking and crisping and working up to the most comforting of sticky pudding dishes.

25g butter, melted

100g pudding/short-grain/risotto rice

2 tablespoons light muscovado sugar

a pinch of freshly grated nutmeg

750ml whole milk

200ml double cream

1 vanilla pod, scored down the middle (some seeds will seep into the cream, but if you like even more vanilla, scrape the seeds out with the back of a spoon and stir through the heated cream)

¼ teaspoon flaked sea salt

favourite jam or stewed fruit, to serve

SERVES

4–6

READY IN

2 HOURS 20 MINS

1. Preheat the oven to 140°C/fan 120°C/gas 1. Melt the butter in a 2 litre heatproof dish or saucepan over a medium heat and add the rice. Stir for a few minutes, until the rice begins to turn translucent. Add the sugar and nutmeg, stir to melt, then add the milk and cream. Bring to the boil. Turn down the heat and add the vanilla pod. Allow the rice and cream to gently simmer for 3 minutes, then stir in the salt.

2. Place in the oven, uncovered, to slowly bake for 2 hours. After this time a crust will have formed and the result will be creamy, thick and golden. Leave for 5 minutes to cool slightly before plunging in with a favourite jam, or stewed fruit.

Bottarga and mussel risotto with crispy chard

COOK TO IMPRESS

The first time I ate this, my husband James had seasoned and crisped up the chard as though it were seaweed, adding even more to the sea-saltiness of the mussels and bottarga. It's an impressive-sounding dish. It tastes sublime. But it's nothing too far from what we know already.

Find bottarga – addictive and delicious cured fish roe – in good Italian delis or by mail from thefishsociety.co.uk. If you can't get it, use thin slices of cured ham for a similar salty kick. But trust me – you'll buy a pack of bottarga and it will go on everything. Eat it in thin slivers with toast, grate it onto pasta or shave it into salads.

a good handful of mussels (300g)
a good splosh of white wine
1 tablespoon olive oil
25g unsalted butter
2 shallots, finely chopped
1 clove of garlic, finely chopped
300g risotto rice (use carnaroli rice this time)
125ml vermouth
a pinch of saffron
750ml–1 litre fish or vegetable stock, heated
a 25g bunch of fresh parsley, leaves and stalks
    separated, both finely chopped
200g chard, stalks finely chopped, leaves thinly
    sliced and washed
vegetable oil, for frying
2 tablespoons crème fraîche
finely grated zest of 1 lemon
bottarga, to serve

SERVES

4–6

TIME TO PREPARE

20 MINUTES

TIME TO COOK

45 MINUTES

1. Pull the beards from the mussels, and discard any that won't close when tapped lightly on the work surface. Heat a large pan over a medium heat and add the mussels and a good splosh of white wine. Cover and simmer for 5–7 minutes, until all the mussels have steamed open. Discard any that are still firmly closed. Cool slightly, then remove the mussels from their shells. Set the meat aside and discard the shells.

2. Melt the oil and half the butter over a gentle heat and add the shallots. Season with salt and pepper and cook for 10–15 minutes, until soft. Add the garlic and cook for another minute or so, then add the rice. Stir for 30 seconds to a minute, then add the vermouth and the saffron. Simmer, stirring, until reduced, then add a ladle of the stock. Stir, simmer, reduce, adding a ladle of stock when necessary, until the rice is just cooked. Add the parsley stalks and chard stalks and the cooked mussels and turn the heat down low. Keep stirring every now and then.

3. Tip 2.5cm of oil into a deep frying pan and put it over a medium-high heat. When hot (throw in a piece of bread and it should sizzle in 40 seconds), add the sliced chard leaves. Fry for a minute, until crisp, then remove to kitchen paper using a slotted spoon.

4. Stir the remaining butter, the crème fraîche, lemon zest and parsley leaves into the risotto (adding a splash more stock if necessary) and check for seasoning. Serve the risotto topped with a handful of the crisp chard and a generous grating of bottarga.

Spicy sausage and radicchio risotto

This is a popular recipe for those who think of a plate of risotto as a flimsy dinner. Allow the sausage to really caramelise in the pan as you fry it – it'll sweeten up the rice, which you'll need to offset the bitter radicchio, and give you crispy, crunchy bits. This is scrumptious with 'nduja too – a very spicy, spreadable Calabrian sausage available from Natoora, Waitrose and Italian delis.

2 tablespoons extra virgin olive oil

50g unsalted butter

8 free-range pork sausages, skin removed

1 onion, finely chopped

1 stick of celery, finely chopped

a good grating of nutmeg

1 teaspoon dried chilli flakes

2 cloves of garlic, finely chopped

350g risotto rice

175ml red wine

700ml–1 litre fresh chicken or
     vegetable stock, heated

1 small head of radicchio, sliced

50g pecorino cheese, grated

toasted breadcrumbs, to serve (optional)

chopped fresh curly-leaf parsley, to serve (optional)

SERVES

4–6

TIME TO PREPARE

15 MINUTES

TIME TO COOK

30 MINUTES

1. Heat the olive oil and half the butter in a large saucepan over a medium-low heat and add the sausage meat. Gently cook for 5–10 minutes, until browned and starting to crisp and caramelise. Then add the onion, celery and nutmeg. Gently fry for 10 minutes, covered, until the onions are very soft and have almost lost their shape. Add the chilli flakes and garlic and stir through, frying for 1 minute.

2. Add the risotto rice and fry for 3 minutes or so, until almost translucent. Turn up the heat and add the red wine, simmering until the alcohol has evaporated and the liquid is absorbed.

3. Pour over a little stock and stir until the rice has absorbed all the liquid again. You should be able to see the bottom of the pan here. Repeat this process, adding a little splash of stock at a time, until the rice is soft. The rice should have a small bite to it. Use more stock or water if it needs more cooking.

4. Add the radicchio and stir through to wilt. Once the rice is cooked and the radicchio has wilted, take the pan off the heat and leave to sit for a minute. Stir in the remaining butter and the pecorino then rest, covered, for 5 minutes. Season well, and serve in shallow bowls. To serve, scatter with crisp breadcrumbs and parsley, if you like.

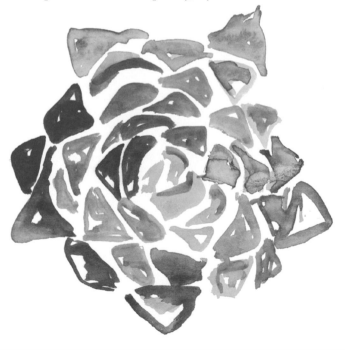

Deep-fried risotto balls

Cooled, sticky risotto holds its shape beautifully and tucks in the soon-to-be molten mozzarella, ready for deep frying. They're greedy and a brilliant hangover cure and I love 'em.

a little olive oil

400g baby spinach leaves, tough stalks removed, leaves washed and dried

400g leftover risotto (baked lemon risotto works well here – see page 70)

10g grated Parmesan cheese

25g good-quality mozzarella cheese, cut into small cubes

sunflower oil, for frying

75g plain flour

2 medium free-range eggs, beaten

50g day-old breadcrumbs or panko breadcrumbs

MAKES

8 BALLS

TIME TO PREPARE

20 MINUTES + CHILLING

TIME TO COOK

10 MINUTES

1. Heat a little olive oil in a large saucepan over a medium heat. Add the spinach leaves in batches until fully wilted. Remove, drain and allow to cool before squeezing out all the excess liquid possible.

2. In a large bowl, mix the leftover risotto with the cooked spinach and the Parmesan. Season generously.

3. Roll 50g of the leftover risotto mix into a ball, then squash flat to make a 5cm circle in the palm of your hand. Place a cube of mozzarella in the centre of the circle, then mould the risotto around it into a bite-size ball, pressing and rubbing the risotto with your finger to weld the open seam. Lay the risotto balls on a plate or baking sheet and leave to chill and set in the fridge for 15 minutes.

4. Meanwhile, heat a pan two-thirds full of sunflower oil over a medium-high heat. Heat to 180°C (check this with a good digital thermometer) or until a 2.5cm cube of bread browns in 40 seconds.

5. While the oil is rising in temperature, place the flour, eggs and breadcrumbs in separate bowls. Remove the risotto balls from the fridge, then coat each one in flour, then egg, then breadcrumbs and set aside on a lined baking tray. Fry 4 at a time for 2–3 minutes, lifting them in and out carefully with a slotted spoon, then lay on kitchen towel to drain the excess oil. Repeat until all the risotto balls are done, then serve sliced open and dunked into a leftover romesco or aioli (see roast chicken, page 102).

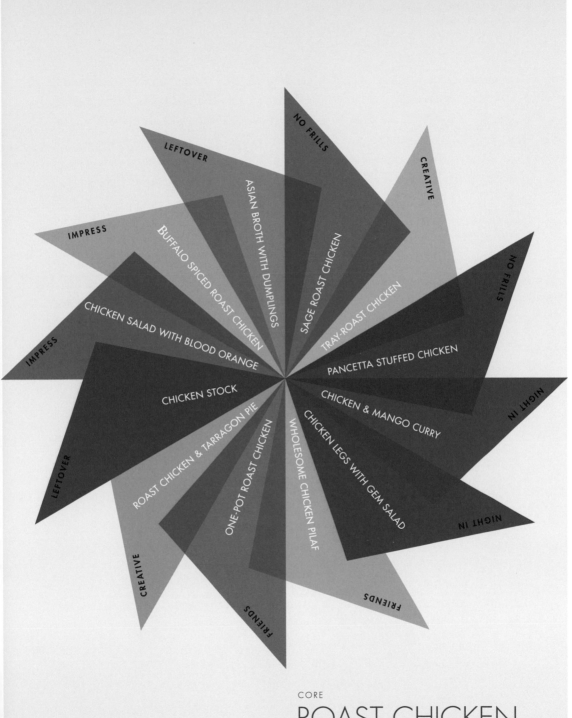

NO FRILLS

CREATIVE

LEFTOVER

IMPRESS

ASIAN BROTH WITH DUMPLINGS

BUFFALO SPICED ROAST CHICKEN

SAGE ROAST CHICKEN

NO FRILLS

IMPRESS

CHICKEN SALAD WITH BLOOD ORANGE

TRAY-ROAST CHICKEN

PANCETTA STUFFED CHICKEN

CHICKEN STOCK

CHICKEN & MANGO CURRY

NIGHT IN

LEFTOVER

ROAST CHICKEN & TARRAGON PIE

ONE-POT ROAST CHICKEN

WHOLESOME CHICKEN PILAF

CHICKEN LEGS WITH GEM SALAD

NIGHT IN

CREATIVE

FRIENDS

FRIENDS

CORE
ROAST CHICKEN

Roast Chicken

There really can be no other recipe that lifts your feet, lightens the spirit and puts warmth in your stomach quite like a garlicky roasted chicken. The smells of herbs, butter and crispy skin flooding from the oven push the senses into overdrive, and with them come yells of 'LUU-UNCHHH' and the stampede of feet. Roast chicken takes little time to prepare and cook, asks for minimal effort and floods us with food memory. It can be flavoured, jointed, stuffed, and leftovers bring infinite possibilities – stock, pilaf, pie – for weekday fodder.

To joint a chicken

1. Ease the legs gently away from the main body, slicing through the skin between the thigh and the body, keeping the knife as close to the body as you can – no need to cut the flesh at this point. Pull the leg out from the body and bend it back on itself. You'll hear a pop and will be able to see the thigh joint exposed from the ball socket. Slice the flesh between the ball and socket to release the leg.

2. Feel and bend the 'knee' joint of the leg – you'll feel a gap in the bone joining the thigh to the drumstick. Slice through the middle – you'll feel no resistance if you go right in between the joint. Repeat with the other leg and thigh. Set aside.

3. Remove the wishbone. Feel for it (a downwards V-shape by the cavity separating the breasts) with your fingers and, using a small, sharp knife, begin to scratch away to reveal the bone. Hook your fingers underneath the wishbone and yank it out.

4. To take the breast and wing off the carcass in one piece, sweep your knife along either side of the breast bone, pulling the skin taut. Slice in sweeping motions as close as possible to the breast bone, cutting the breast meat back from the neck to the cavity. Cut through the wing joint to remove the breast and wing, cutting away any excess skin and flesh. Do the same on the other side.

5. To portion the breasts and wings, fold the wing up on to the breast. Using the wing as your guide, slice off two-thirds of the breast in one piece. You will now have 2 wings and with a bit of breast, 2 small portions of breast, 2 drumsticks and 2 thighs.

Tips for perfect roast chicken

- Make sure your bird is at room temperature – it loosens up the meat (like resting after cooking) and makes for a juicier roast.

- Lift your chicken up on its legs as though it were standing. This way you'll get a better idea of where everything is – tail between legs, neck between wings, etc. – for when you're stuffing or jointing the bird.

- A 1.8kg chicken will serve a generous 4 or be just enough for 6 people. I often find it easier to carve the whole chicken and serve it from a platter to judge how much meat everyone can have. Keep the scraps for the week ahead's meals.

- A note about free-range: If you want to have a great-tasting chicken, go free-range. Free-range chickens walk about, flap their wings and have more space to move, unlike boxed-in chooks. Their meat is firmer, juicier and won't pap in your mouth. They have a better flavour and a better life than a £2 chicken.

- As long as you begin with a room-temperature bird and start the oven at a high temperature, roasting a 1.8kg chicken for just over an hour will give you deliciously succulent meat – it will be cooked perfectly. For every 450g of chicken after that, add 15–20 minutes to the cooking time. Wrap it tightly with foil and cover with a tea towel to insulate for 15 minutes after roasting.

- The internal temperature of a well-cooked chicken should be between 65°C and 70°C – at this temperature the pink haemoglobin will break down and the juices will turn clear. If the meat is just a little pink, it's fine! If the meat can be pulled easily off the bone and the juices are clear, you're good to go. If it's very pink, still bouncy and the juices are cloudy and pink, put it back in for 10 minutes. When poking with a skewer or thermometer, only pierce the thigh meat away from the bone for a more precise reading.

Roast chicken

CORE

When I have the pleasure of eating a plump roasted chicken that is juicy and tender, and the skin is crisp, most other chicken recipes become redundant and dull. Cooking it pure, with a little boost from garlic and lemon, is truly the most delicious way. As Diana Henry wrote in *Food from Plenty*, 'There's nothing like a roast chicken to make you feel hungry, happy and cared for.'

When I can't help but play a bit with seasoning or jazz up the chicken to suit the occasion, I always work from the core recipe. Keep to four simple guidelines and you'll have yourself a marvellous roast:

1. Use lots of butter or oil.

2. Season well.

3. Keep your chook at room temperature.

4. Don't be tempted to overcook it – it can go back in if still a bit pink and can rest for a long time, but you can't bring it back.

25g softened unsalted butter

2 cloves of garlic, crushed (with the back of a knife or a crusher)

1 x 1.8kg free-range chicken, at room temperature

½ a lemon

a bunch of fresh thyme

1 tablespoon plain flour

150ml chicken stock or water

100ml white wine

SERVES

4–6 WITH LEFTOVERS

TIME TO PREPARE

10 MINUTES

TIME TO COOK

1 HOUR 15 MINS

1. Preheat the oven to 200°C/fan 180°C/gas 6. In a small bowl, mash together the butter and garlic, with generous pinches of sea salt and black pepper.

2. Gently loosen the skin from the neck (the bit between the wings) of the chicken using your fingers, then slide the softened butter all the way up the breast, delicately massaging the skin to smooth it out. Try not to tear the skin. Smooth a little butter over the top of the skin and season again.

3. Push the lemon and thyme bunch up the neck cavity. Place the chicken into a large roasting tray and slide into the hot oven. After 15 minutes of skin crisping, turn the oven down the oven to 180°C/fan 160°C/gas 4 and roast for another hour, spooning the roasting juices over the chicken halfway through cooking.

4. Check that your bird is properly cooked by piercing the thickest part of the thigh with a skewer or a small sharp knife. If the juices run clear, it is cooked (see introduction opposite); if they are still pink and cloudy, put it back in for another 5–10 minutes. Remove the chicken from the oven and cover tightly with foil and a tea towel to insulate. Let the chicken rest like this for 15 minutes before carving.

5. The juices from the chicken taste so good on their own that you may decide not to make a gravy. If you want the juices to go further, tip the resting juices from the roasting tin into a pan over a medium-high heat and bring to a simmer. Add the flour to make a light roux and, with a wooden spoon, scrape in any crispy chicken remnants that are stuck to the pan. Gradually pour in the stock and wine as it thickens and bring to the boil, stirring all the while until the alcohol has evaporated and the gravy has reduced to your desired thickness and flavour. Season well and strain into a warm jug, ready to pour, hot, over carved chicken.

Sage roast chicken

NO FRILLS

Very rarely do I roast a chicken without dousing or stuffing the skin with oil or butter. Push and spread garlic butter under the skin and over the breast and follow with sage leaves. The leaves will fry and become visible as the skin crisps, and give out the most intoxicating smell as the chicken cooks. Best of all, the scented juices will run into the tin for a perfectly seasoned gravy.

25g softened unsalted butter
2 cloves of garlic, crushed
1 x 1.8kg free-range chicken, at room temperature
6 fresh sage leaves

1. Preheat the oven to 200°C/fan 180°C/gas 6. In a small bowl, mash together the butter and garlic, with generous pinches of sea salt and black pepper. Gently loosen the skin from the neck of the bird using your fingers, then slide the garlicky butter all the way up the breast, delicately massaging the skin to smooth it out – try not to rip the skin. Follow with the sage leaves, so they sit flat against the breast.

2. Place the chicken in a large roasting tray and slide into the hot oven. After 15 minutes, turn down the oven to 180°C/fan 160°C/gas 4 and roast the chicken for another hour, basting it with its juices halfway through, until the skin is crisp and the juices run clear.

3. Cover the cooked bird tightly in foil and insulate with a tea towel. Rest for 15 minutes before carving.

SERVES	TIME TO PREPARE	TIME TO COOK
4–6 WITH LEFTOVERS	10 MINUTES	1 HOUR 15 MINS

Tray-roast chicken with cherry tomatoes and crushed potatoes

GET CREATIVE

Give jointing a go (see tips, page 92), or ask your butcher to do it for you. Otherwise, buy ready-butchered drumsticks and thighs.

Crispy skin, crackle and crunch is crucial, so before the wine goes in, give the chicken a head-start in the pan to get golden. No need to chop anything (apart from the lemons) until it reaches the plate.

1 x 1.8kg free-range chicken, jointed into 8
3 tablespoons olive oil
16–20 baby new potatoes, left whole (or halved if using larger new pots)
1 lemon, cut into wedges
6 cloves of garlic, just crushed, skins left on
20 cherry tomatoes on the vine
a small handful of fresh rosemary sprigs
100ml white wine

1. Preheat the oven to 200°C/fan 180°C/gas 6. Season the chicken skin well with salt and pepper. Heat 1 tablespoon of the olive oil in a large frying pan over a medium-high heat and fry the chicken pieces, skin-side down, for 7 minutes, until crisp and golden. Remove from the heat and set aside.

2. Bring a large pan of salted water to the boil and add the new potatoes. Cook for 7–10 minutes to par-boil, then drain well and transfer to a deep roasting tin. Squash the potatoes slightly with the bottom of a heavy pan or masher, then toss with the remaining 2 tablespoons of olive oil, the lemon wedges and the garlic. Season generously.

3. Place the chicken pieces on top with the vine cherry tomatoes and rosemary sprigs. Pour over the wine and roast in the oven for 35 minutes, until the chicken is cooked through and the potatoes are crisp and sizzling.

SERVES	TIME TO PREPARE	TIME TO COOK
4–6	15 MINUTES	50 MINUTES

Pancetta and onion stuffed chicken

A hidden pocket for even more flavour; the herby, salty stuffing marinates and seasons the whole chicken during cooking, and, when sliced into, makes a delicious accompaniment to the meat. Stuffing a chicken makes a roast go further, and is a rewarding way of using up loose ends from the fridge.

Pork and chicken are delicious together. Mum always drapes bacon on to the skin to crisp up during cooking or throws chipolatas into the bottom of the roasting tin. Here, the porky goodness is locked inside.

1 x 1.8kg free-range chicken, at room temperature
5 rashers of pancetta, chopped
a little olive oil
2 shallots, very finely chopped
25g unsalted butter, softened
3 cloves of garlic, crushed
a large handful of fresh parsley leaves,
    finely chopped
1 free-range egg yolk
20g day-old breadcrumbs

1. Preheat the oven to 200°C/fan 180°C/gas 6. Fry the pancetta in a small pan over a medium heat with a little olive oil for 5 minutes, until crisp. Transfer to kitchen paper to drain and add the shallots to the pan, frying for a further 10 minutes until softened. Stir in the garlic and fry for another minute. Leave to cool.

2. In a bowl, combine the pancetta, chopped parsley, egg yolk and breadcrumbs. Stir in the cooled onions and garlic and season well with sea salt and black pepper.

SERVES

4–6 WITH LEFTOVERS

TIME TO PREPARE

20 MINUTES

TIME TO COOK

1 HOUR 15 MINS

3. Gently loosen the skin from the neck of the bird, using your fingers, then slide the butter all the way up the breast, delicately massaging the skin to smooth it out and trying not to rip the skin.

4. Loosen the skin at the base of the breasts, between the legs. There'll be a flap of skin which you'll use to hold the stuffing in. Push 4 tablespoons of the stuffing a quarter of the way up under the skin of the breast. You want it to sit at the tip of the breasts nearest to the roasting tray. Gently pull the loose skin over the stuffing and tuck it under the base of the bird.

5. Place the chicken in a large roasting tray and slide into the hot oven. After 15 minutes, turn the heat down to 180°C/fan 160°C/gas 4 and roast the chicken for another hour, basting it with its juices halfway through cooking. Check that the juices run clear by piercing the thigh with a skewer.

6. Remove the chicken from the oven, pour off the juices into a pan to make a gravy, and cover tightly with foil and a tea towel for 15 minutes. When ready to carve, slice off the stuffing and serve alongside the crisp chicken on a serving platter.

Other stuffing ideas:

- Squeeze the meat from sausages and mix with chopped fresh cranberries, chopped fresh parsley and chopped ready-roasted chestnuts.

- Mix ground almonds with finely chopped blanched whole almonds and a little olive oil. Stir in chopped roasted peppers and chopped fresh rosemary leaves. Add a little paprika too, if you like, for a kick.

- Fry very finely chopped cooking chorizo until crisp, allow to cool, then mix with the zest of a lemon, a small handful of fresh breadcrumbs and finely grated Manchego cheese to bind.

- Simply whiz fresh parsley, sage, thyme and rosemary together in a blender and mix with softened butter and garlic.

Chicken and mango curry

A whole roast chicken on the weekend may be the best answer to a cheap week ahead. Meat, being the most expensive ingredient of the week's shop, often means scrimping on other goodnesses that can make cooking more fun. Not so, here. Roast two chooks for Sunday supper, let the skin crinkle and cool on one, and shred it of every little scrap. Use the meat well and you'll find you can make it go far with just a few punchy partnering flavours.

Curry is my favourite go-to for zapping up loose ends. Spice thickens sauces, enhances flavour; nuts give extra protein and texture and fill you up; herbs and lime freshen up the chicken; and the mango – well, it's a heavenly accompaniment to chicken and easily brightens up the plate.

If using fresh chicken, chop 200g of thigh meat into 2cm chunks and add to the pan after you bring the stock to the boil.

Or drizzle whole bone-in thighs with olive oil, season, roast for 35 minutes at 180°C/fan 160°C/gas 4, then shred into the curry.

a 4cm knob of fresh root ginger, peeled and
    roughly chopped
1 stick of lemongrass, peeled of its woody outer
    layer and finely sliced
2 cloves of garlic
½–1 red chilli (measure its heat by snipping the tip
    off and holding it against your tongue)
1 tablespoon groundnut oil
200g leftover thigh, leg and breast meat from a
    roasted free-range chicken, or 200g fresh
    chicken (see introduction)
160ml coconut cream
1 tablespoon fish sauce
1 ripe mango, peeled and chopped
a large bunch of fresh coriander, chopped
1 lime
3 spring onions, sliced
2 tablespoons toasted cashew nuts,
    roughly chopped

SERVES

2

READY IN

20 MINUTES

1. Whiz the ginger, lemongrass, garlic and chilli in a blender or very finely chop to a paste. Heat the groundnut oil in a frying pan over a medium-low heat and fry the paste for 2 minutes, until fragrant.

2. Add the leftover chicken (or fresh chicken, see introduction) and stir to coat in the spices. Stir in the coconut cream and fish sauce and simmer gently for 10 minutes.

3. Just before serving, stir in the mango and chopped coriander. Squeeze in the juice from the lime and serve topped with the spring onions, cashew nuts and with some fluffy basmati rice.

Chicken legs with gem salad, aioli and lightly pickled red onion

NIGHT IN

Crispy chicken, dunked into this smooth, garlic sauce, topped with sweet onion and scooped up with gem lettuce leaves. No cutlery needed, but lots of licking fingers and napkins tucked into shirts.

Legs roasted on their own take less time than a whole bird. The same rules apply, though: butter generously, season well, and roast to crisp.

To carve the legs from the breast, ease back the skin with a sharp knife without tearing the flesh, then fold the legs back until the joint pops from the socket. Slice straight through the joint. Alternatively buy the legs already butchered.

1 tablespoon olive oil
2 free-range chicken legs (thigh and drumstick), skin on, butter rubbed under the skin, skin sprinkled with flaked sea salt
100ml white wine
2 sprigs of fresh rosemary

FOR THE PICKLED ONION
(they keep for up to 3 weeks in an airtight jar in the fridge)
1 red onion, finely sliced
1 teaspoon flaked sea salt
1 teaspoon granulated sugar
2 tablespoons white wine vinegar
a bunch of fresh tarragon, leaves only

FOR THE AIOLI
2 free-range egg yolks (not too fresh), at room temperature
1 large clove of garlic, crushed with flaked sea salt
a small splash of white wine vinegar
100ml light-coloured and mild-flavoured olive oil
a squeeze of lemon juice

SERVES

1–2

TIME TO PREPARE

20 MINUTES

TIME TO COOK

40 MINUTES

1 teaspoon caster sugar

1 teaspoon Dijon mustard

1 tablespoon red wine vinegar

3 tablespoons good extra virgin olive oil

a squeeze of lemon juice

1 baby gem lettuce, washed and dried

1. Preheat the oven to 180°C/fan 160°C/gas 4. Heat the tablespoon of olive oil in a wide frying pan over a medium-high heat. Fry the chicken skin-side down for 5–7 minutes, until the skin is really crisp and golden. Transfer to a roasting tin, pour in the wine and add the rosemary. Cover with foil, and slide into the oven for 35–40 minutes, until cooked through and moist.

2. Mix the sliced onion with the salt, sugar and vinegar and leave to lightly souse for 1 hour. They'll be bright pink, soft and slightly sharp. Drain and toss with the tarragon.

3. Meanwhile, make the aioli. Whisk the egg yolks with the garlic and vinegar in a bowl. Slowly and gradually, drop by drop, pour in the olive oil, continuously whisking, until you have a thick, creamy mayonnaise (you may not need all of the oil – rescue with a drop of water if it's too thick for your liking). Season with salt and pepper and the lemon juice.

4. When the chicken is cooked through, remove it from the oven and allow it to rest for 15 minutes, covered with foil and a tea towel.

5. While the chicken is resting, prepare the gem salad: whisk the sugar with the mustard and vinegar until the sugar has dissolved. Gradually whisk in the olive oil until thick, the stir in the lemon juice. Toss with the lettuce.

6. Serve the chicken legs warm or cold, with the aioli, pickled onions and the dressed gem lettuce. A perfect bite for one or two. Get messy.

Wholesome chicken pilaf

Chicken thighs give the most flavoursome meat on the chicken. Opt for these over breast every time if shredding into salads with bold ingredients. Pilafs are good fodder for any time of year, but especially served outside, alongside a barbecue. Shred the meat and build layers through the rice – add crisp almonds, juicy pomegranate seeds or fresh cherries, fresh herbs, tart lemon zest and plenty of spice.

Brown rice gives chew and a nutty flavour, and holds its shape when cooked for longer in stock. If you're not a fan of brown rice or are short of time but still want the wholegrain taste, use a gluten-free bulgur wheat or barley couscous.

If using bought free-range chicken thighs, preheat the oven to 180°C/fan 160°C/gas 4. Drizzle the chicken thighs with olive oil and season well. Put on a roasting tray and roast in the oven for 35 minutes, then remove to rest. Shred from the bone when cool and toss into the rice with any roasting juices.

2 tablespoons olive oil, plus extra for drizzling
2 red onions, finely sliced
1 tablespoon light brown sugar
2 tablespoons Chinese five-spice
5 cardamom pods, slashed
1 clove of garlic, finely sliced
350g brown rice
1 litre good-quality chicken stock
250g leftover meat from your roast chicken,
*   or 4 cooked chicken thighs (see introduction)*
4 tablespoons chopped pistachio nuts, to serve
4 tablespoons flaked almonds, toasted, to serve
100g pomegranate seeds, to serve
grated zest and juice of 1 lemon, to serve
a large handful of fresh parsley leaves,
*   roughly chopped, to serve*
a large handful of fresh mint leaves,
*   roughly chopped, to serve*

1. Heat the olive oil in a large saucepan over a medium-low heat and add the onions. Sprinkle over the sugar and gently fry for 10–15 minutes, until soft and starting to caramelise, then add the five-spice, cardamom and garlic and fry for 1 minute more. Add the rice and stir to coat.

2. Pour in the stock and bring to the boil, then simmer gently, covered, for 30 minutes, until the rice has absorbed the liquid and is tender. Remove the lid and season well.

3. Add the chicken to the rice and stir through. Transfer to a large serving bowl or plate and top with the pistachios, almonds, pomegranate seeds, lemon zest and juice, and herbs. Toss through with extra olive oil to serve. Season again to taste.

SERVES	TIME TO PREPARE	TIME TO COOK
4–6	20 MINUTES	45 MINUTES

One-pot roast chicken, cannellini and chorizo with romesco sauce

The bung-it-all-in method. Everything goes into the pot and bubbles away together, sharing flavours, textures and juices. It's a favourite for nights when you just want to bathe, read, and wait for the timer to ping for dinner. Pile on the sweet, spicy romesco. It's moreishly rich and stirs into the gravy with extra wahoomph – you can make it up to 1 week ahead and store it in an airtight jar.

Experiment here – use large pieces of pancetta and haricot beans instead of chorizo and cannellini, or add cleaned clams from stage 6 to steam open. For a veggie version, pot-roast a large pumpkin, peeled and sliced into 6, instead of the chicken.

a knob of softened unsalted butter
1 x 1.8kg free-range chicken, at room temperature
1 tablespoon olive oil
4 small cooking chorizo sausages, chopped (Unearthed are good)

6 shallots, peeled and left whole (to peel shallots easily, sit them in a bowl of just-boiled water for 5 minutes, then drain, refresh and remove skins)
2 leeks, washed, drained, quartered and sliced lengthways
12 baby carrots, peeled
175ml white wine
400ml chicken stock
2 sprigs of fresh rosemary
2 bay leaves
3 x 400g tins of cannellini beans, drained and rinsed

FOR THE ROMESCO SAUCE
(MAKES 300G)
50g ground almonds
1–2 large cloves of garlic, crushed
50g stale breadcrumbs (1 chunky slice of stale bread, whizzed)
1 large tomato, peeled (score a cross in the bottom of the tomato and, like the shallots, blanch in just-boiled water for a few minutes, then peel back and remove the skins)
2 large roasted red peppers from a jar, well-drained
1 tablespoon red wine vinegar
4 tablespoons extra virgin olive oil

1. Preheat the oven to 200°C/fan 180°C/gas 6. Rub the butter under the skin of the chicken and season with salt and pepper. Heat the olive oil in a casserole dish or ovenproof saucepan large enough to fit the chicken plus a bit more, over a medium-high heat. Add the chorizo and fry for 5 minutes until crisp, then remove with a slotted spoon on to kitchen paper and set aside.

2. Turn the heat down and add the whole shallots, leeks and carrots to the chorizo oil left in the pan. Fry for 5 minutes, until just beginning to soften, then return the chorizo to the pan and add the wine. Bring to the boil and simmer for 3 minutes, until the alcohol has evaporated.

3. Add the stock, rosemary and bay leaves and bring to the boil. Turn down to a simmer and place the chicken on top of the vegetables. Slide the dish into the oven and roast, uncovered, for 15 minutes so the skin can colour. Baste the chicken with the juices, then place a lid on the dish and roast for a further hour.

4. Meanwhile, make the romesco sauce. Whiz the ground almonds, crushed garlic and breadcrumbs together in a food processor until well combined. Add the tomato, roasted peppers and red wine vinegar and blitz until you have a rough paste. Gradually add the olive oil, still whizzing, to make a smooth, bright-red sauce. Season and set aside.

5. Remove the dish from the oven and transfer the chicken to a carving board. Allow it to rest for 15 minutes, covered with foil and a tea towel.

6. While the bird is resting, return the dish to the hob (it will be hot!). Add the beans, season, then simmer uncovered for 5 minutes, until the beans are warmed through and the sauce can reduce a little.

7. Carve the bird and spoon over the juicy cannellini beans and chorizo. Serve with the romesco and a crunchy green salad.

SERVES	TIME TO PREPARE	TIME TO COOK
4–6	25 MINUTES	2 HOURS

Roast chicken, ham, leek and tarragon pie

GET CREATIVE

Oh, dear pie, how you have a habit of making us happy … It's something about the bubbling, creamy sauce, the crisp pastry topping and that glorious line of almost sodden pastry that never fails to please.

Most of the time, I'll make this pie using leftovers. This is a great one for a Monday night after a Sunday roast. It's also good for using up leftover turkey on Boxing Day. You can tear up the leftover morsels from a cooked bird and throw in other odds and ends from the fridge. This pie freezes really well – wrap it up in greaseproof and foil, freeze, then defrost thoroughly to reheat.

1 x 1.8kg free-range chicken, at room temperature (or 300g leftover chicken meat)
30g softened unsalted butter, plus extra for greasing
2 large leeks, thoroughly rinsed and finely sliced into rounds
2 medium carrots, peeled and roughly chopped
a good glug of white wine
300ml fresh stock (chicken, turkey or ham)
150ml double cream
2 tablespoons wholegrain mustard
2 tablespoons Dijon mustard
100g leftover roast ham, shredded
a small bunch of fresh tarragon, finely chopped
plain flour, for dusting
200g all-butter puff pastry, chilled (I like to roll from a block rather than using ready-rolled pastry – this goes for shortcrust too)
1 free-range egg yolk, for glazing

1. Preheat the oven to 200°C/fan 180°C/gas 6. Rub your bird under the skin with 5g of the butter and season well. Place on a roasting tray and slide it into the oven. After 15 minutes, turn the oven down to 180°C/fan 160°C/gas 4 and roast for another hour, until cooked through and the juices run clear. Cover with foil and a tea towel and leave to rest for 15 minutes.

SERVES

4–6

TIME TO PREPARE

20 MINUTES + COOLING

TIME TO COOK

1 HOUR 40 MINS

2. Meanwhile, butter a 2 litre ovenproof dish. Melt the butter in a saucepan over a medium heat and add the leeks and carrots. Fry for 10–15 minutes, until soft. Pour in the white wine, turn up the heat, and simmer for 5 minutes to evaporate the alcohol. Add the stock and simmer for 10–15 minutes to reduce by two-thirds, then add the cream and mustards. Simmer until the sauce is syrupy and thick. Add the ham and tarragon, season to taste, then pour into the ovenproof dish. Set aside to cool (you can make the filling the day before).

3. When the chicken is ready, remove it from the oven – leave the oven turned on – and allow the chicken to cool slightly before shredding the meat from the carcass (keep the bones for stock). You want about 300g of shredded chicken for the pie – save the rest for tomorrow's lunch. Mix the chicken into the dish of sauce.

4. Roll out the pastry on a floured surface to the thickness of a £1 coin and to a little larger than your dish. Cut some of the trimmings to line the edge of the dish and make a platform for the pie to sit on (save some for decoration). Brush with some of the egg yolk. Lift the pastry with a rolling pin and gently place it on top of the brushed edges, pressing down the edges – crimping if you like – with your index finger.

5. Lightly brush the pastry with the rest of the egg yolk, then top with cut-out shapes from the rest of the pastry trimmings and brush with more egg. Place the pie on a baking sheet and slide it into the oven. Bake for 25 minutes, or until the pastry is golden, puffed and crisp, and the sauce is bubbling. Serve with blanched and buttered spring greens or sprouts.

More scrumptious chicken pie fillings

- Fry chunkily chopped chorizo in a pan until crisp and golden. Make a roux with half cider, half stock. Add a dash of cream and stir in shredded chicken.

- Roast diced pumpkin with garlic and olive oil. Mix with chillies, wilted spinach and roasted chicken, then stir into a creamy roux. Top with crumpled sheets of filo pastry and brush with milk or oil before baking.

- Soak dried morels (and/or porcini) in hot water for at least 2 hours. Strain, reserving the liquid, and rinse under water. Fry with butter and thyme and stir in cream and some of the soaking liquid. Bubble down by half and season. Stir in shredded chicken.

- Mix shredded cooked chicken with spring onions, chopped, grilled artichokes, blanched asparagus and peas and mix with a loose chicken stock roux. Top with almond pastry (roll flaked almonds into the pastry or make your own shortcrust with half ground almonds, half flour).

Chicken stock

LEFTOVER LOVE

Because if you've got a chicken carcass going, why wouldn't you? Use it for all the soups in this book and for your chicken dumpling broth. Freeze in batches for up to 3 months, and defrost when needed.

1 raw or roasted chicken carcass
2 sticks of celery, roughly chopped
1 onion, quartered
2 large carrots, peeled and roughly chopped
½ a bulb of garlic (the whole bulb,
    sliced across the middle)
4 black peppercorns
2 bay leaves
6 sprigs of fresh thyme
2 sprigs of fresh rosemary

1. Put the stripped chicken carcass into a large pot with 2 litres of water, the vegetables, garlic, peppercorns and herbs. Bring to the boil, then cover and turn down the heat to a gentle simmer. Simmer for 2½–3 hours.

2. Leave the stock to cool, then strain and divide between smaller lidded containers. Discard the debris. Leave in the fridge in an airtight container for up to 10 days, freeze for up to 3 months, or use immediately for poaching, making sauces and soups.

MAKES	TIME TO PREPARE	TIME TO COOK
1 LITRE	12 MINUTES	2 HOURS 30 MINS

Chicken salad with blood orange and giant couscous

COOK TO IMPRESS

Salads give an enormous amount of wiggle-room when it comes to making a roast chicken go further. They give scope to experiment with ingredients, and it's often when whisking the dressing that I decide to add a little of something else to the bowl. Here it was pumpkin seeds. Roast chicken seems to live very happily alongside crunchy nuts and tiny seeds – they give oiliness, texture and are subtle enough in flavour not to overpower – they are a sprinkle-on, effortless addition to any salad.

Ras el hanout is a blend of spices used in Moroccan cooking and gives a wonderful fragrance to the chicken – the smell when it's roasting will send you into a stupor. It is easy to get hold of – Bart sell a tin – but it's just as easy to make your own and keep it in the cupboard to stir into tagines, dressings, roast lamb or soups.

SERVES

4–6

TIME TO PREPARE

20 MINUTES

TIME TO COOK

1 HOUR 15 MINS

TO MAKE RAS EL HANOUT

2 teaspoons ground ginger

2 teaspoons ground cardamom seeds

2 teaspoons ground mace

1 teaspoon ground cinnamon

1 teaspoon ground allspice

1 teaspoon coriander seeds

1 teaspoon freshly grated nutmeg

1 teaspoon ground turmeric

½ teaspoon black peppercorns

½ teaspoon white peppercorns

½ teaspoon cayenne pepper

1 star anise

¼ teaspoon ground cloves

Put all the ingredients into a pestle and mortar or a spice grinder and grind to a fine powder. Store in an airtight jar – it will keep up to 6 months.

1 x 1.8kg free-range chicken, at room temperature

3 cloves of garlic, crushed

3 tablespoons ras el hanout (see introduction)

20g softened unsalted butter

2 blood oranges, 1 peeled and finely sliced,
    1 unpeeled and halved

300g giant couscous

4 large handfuls of lamb's lettuce and little leaves

2 tablespoons chopped fresh parsley leaves

2 tablespoons pumpkin seeds

FOR THE DRESSING

1 tablespoon pomegranate molasses, or 180ml
    pomegranate juice, simmered and reduced
    to 2 tablespoons (find pomegranate molasses
    at thespiceshop.co.uk, or buy Al Rabih Pome
    granate Molasses from Sainsbury's and
    Middle Eastern shops)

1 tablespoon red wine vinegar

50ml rapeseed oil

2 tablespoons natural Greek yoghurt

1. Preheat the oven to 200°C/fan 180°C/gas 6. Place the chicken in a large roasting tray. Mix the garlic with the ras el hanout and combine with the softened butter. Push some of the butter mix under the skin of the chicken, being careful not to tear the skin, and smooth out with your fingers across the breast. Rub the rest of the bird with the remaining butter and season generously with salt and pepper. Push half the unpeeled orange into the cavity.

2. Slide the chicken into the oven. After 15 minutes, turn the oven down to 180°C/fan 160°C/gas 4 and cook for a further hour, basting with the juices every so often until cooked.

3. While the chicken is cooking, cook the couscous. Bring a pan of water to the boil and add the giant couscous. Simmer for 7–10 minutes, or according to the packet instructions, until tender. Drain and rinse under cold water. Set aside.

4. When the juices of the chicken run clear, remove the bird from the oven, transfer to a carving board and leave to rest for 15 minutes, covered with foil and a tea towel. Drain off any juices from the chicken and reserve for drizzling over the salad with the dressing. Slice up the chicken and set aside.

5. For the dressing, mix the pomegranate molasses or reduced pomegranate juice and red wine vinegar together. Slowly whisk in the rapeseed oil until the dressing emulsifies, then stir in the yoghurt. Season well with salt and pepper to taste.

6. Assemble the leaves, parsley, giant couscous and remaining sliced orange in a large shallow salad bowl and top with the spiced chicken. Drizzle over the dressing liberally, along with the reserved chicken juices, and top with the pumpkin seeds.

Buffalo spiced roast chicken with blue cheese dressing and smoky sauce

Inspired by the happy onslaught of US-style cooking in the UK, this recipe uses a combination of warming spices and sticky honey and waves a vague, tenuous salute to a Bloody Mary. First thoughts are to sticky ribs (for which you can use the same rub, but stir in treacle instead of honey and make a larger amount for more stick), then to moreish, spicy chicken wings, then to jazzing up a whole bird. Spicing the butter before you rub it into the skin is a brilliant way of bringing heat and flavour to the meat. Pierce a few holes in the breasts and legs for the spices to seep into the chicken while it marinates. The blue cheese dressing is madly addictive and there's extra hot sauce too, for more punch.

If you feel like getting even more creative, try these two roasting techniques:

Spatchcock: If you have a barbecue burning, turn the chicken over, cut down the backbone with scissors and flatten the bird out to spatchcock it. This will cook the bird evenly but will also look fantastic! This works for the oven too.

Beer-can chicken: Empty half the beer from a can into a glass (to drink), then carefully place the chicken over the can, so that the chicken is sitting upright, with the can in the cavity. Roast the bird upright in a roasting tray in the oven – the beer will steam through the meat and make the most deliciously moist chicken.

SERVES	TIME TO PREPARE	TIME TO COOK
4–6	20 MINUTES + MARINATING	1 HOUR 15 MINS

2 tablespoons extra virgin olive oil

3 tablespoons Tabasco

2 teaspoons cayenne pepper

1 tablespoon runny honey

2 tablespoons tomato ketchup

1 teaspoon Worcestershire sauce

½ teaspoon ground cloves

2 cloves of garlic, crushed

1 x 1.8kg free-range chicken, at room temperature

FOR THE SMOKY SAUCE

2 tablespoons hot sauce (Cholula is good)

2 tablespoons Tabasco

a pinch of smoked paprika

1 tablespoon red wine vinegar

FOR THE BLUE CHEESE DRESSING

150g blue cheese (St Agur)

4 tablespoons soured cream

½ a bunch of fresh chives, finely snipped,
plus a few to serve

1. For the chicken marinade, mix the olive oil, Tabasco, cayenne pepper, honey, ketchup, Worcestershire sauce, ground cloves and garlic. Season well, then push the marinade up and under the skin and massage into the rest of the bird. Marinate in a roasting tin for an hour at room temperature or overnight in the fridge. Bring the chicken to room temperature once you've taken it out of the fridge.

2. Preheat the oven to 200°C/fan 180°C/gas 6 and slide the chicken into the oven. After 15 minutes turn down the heat to 180°C/fan 160°C/gas 4 and roast the chicken for a further hour, basting halfway through cooking with the roasting juices. If the spices start to burn, cover the chicken with foil, but you want it to be crisp and blackened. Remove the chicken from the oven and set aside to rest, covered with foil and a tea towel, for 15 minutes.

3. Meanwhile, mix the ingredients for the blue cheese dressing in a bowl. Season to taste and top with a few extra chives.

4. Heat the sauce ingredients in a saucepan over a medium heat and simmer for 5 minutes. Season and transfer to a bowl to serve. Carve up the chicken and serve with the smoky sauce, blue cheese dressing and a crunchy salad.

Asian-style broth with dumplings

LEFTOVER LOVE

There tend to be about 100 wrappers in one pack of wontons, which means – joy – scrambling for new, inventive ways to fill them. It doesn't just have to be chicken that you fill them with – the first time I cooked these it was leftover guinea fowl and scraggy, bruised mushrooms that had hung over from Sunday lunch. You can make dumplings into the most beautiful shapes. Stuff them with leftover chicken, crimp the edges to the top, fry in oil on one side, then quickly blanch in boiling water for a bowlful of gyoza.

One tip: Make sure your filling is not too wet, or it will steam the pastry open.

FOR THE DUMPLINGS

150g leftover chicken, roughly chopped

2 teaspoons sesame oil

1 teaspoon fish sauce

½ teaspoon rice wine vinegar

1 spring onion, chopped

12–14 wonton wrappers

FOR THE BROTH

1 litre fresh, homemade chicken stock (see page 110)

2½ tablespoons fish sauce

1 tablespoon mirin rice wine

1 tablespoon soy sauce

2 star anise

a thumb-sized knob of fresh root ginger, peeled and finely sliced

1 red chilli, finely sliced at an angle, plus extra to serve

5 shiitake mushrooms, sliced

3 spring onions, sliced

SERVES	TIME TO PREPARE	TIME TO COOK
2	20 MINUTES	25 MINUTES

1. Put all the dumpling ingredients except the wonton wrappers into a food processor and blitz to a rough paste. Transfer to a small bowl, cover and set aside.

2. Heat the chicken stock in a medium-sized saucepan over a medium heat. Add the fish sauce, rice wine and soy sauce and bring to the boil. Turn down the heat and add the star anise, ginger and chilli. Cook on a low simmer for 10 minutes, so all the flavours can infuse.

3. Meanwhile, assemble the dumplings. Lay a dumpling wrapper in the palm of your hand and place a heaped teaspoon of the filling in the centre. Fold up the sides around the filling to form a flower shape. Pinch to bind, using a drop of water if necessary. Place on a lightly floured surface and continue until all the mixture has been used.

4. Drop the dumplings into the simmering broth along with the shiitake mushrooms and cook for 2 minutes, until the mushrooms have wilted slightly, the pastry is soft and they are hot all the way through – they will float to the top of the pan. Ladle the broth into two bowls and divide the dumplings between them. Scatter with the spring onions and the extra red chilli. Serve with cold beer and extra soy sauce.

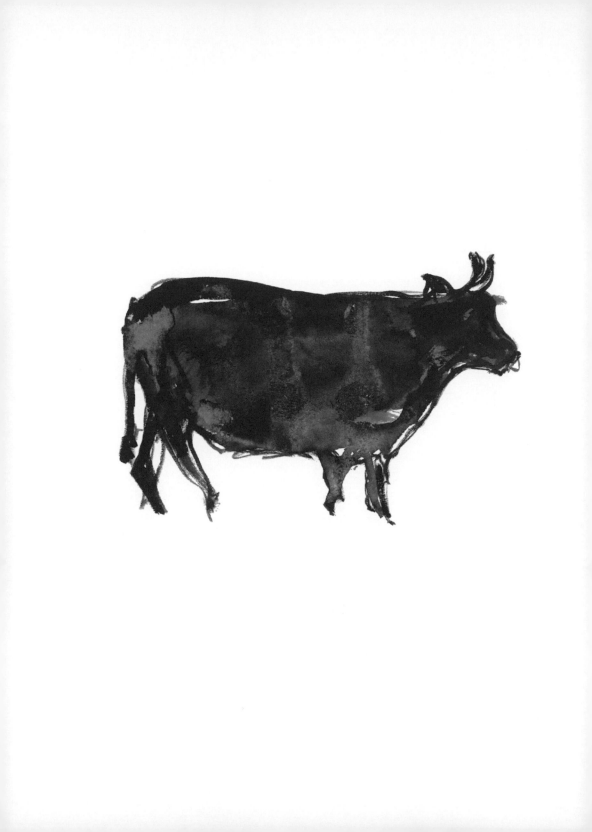

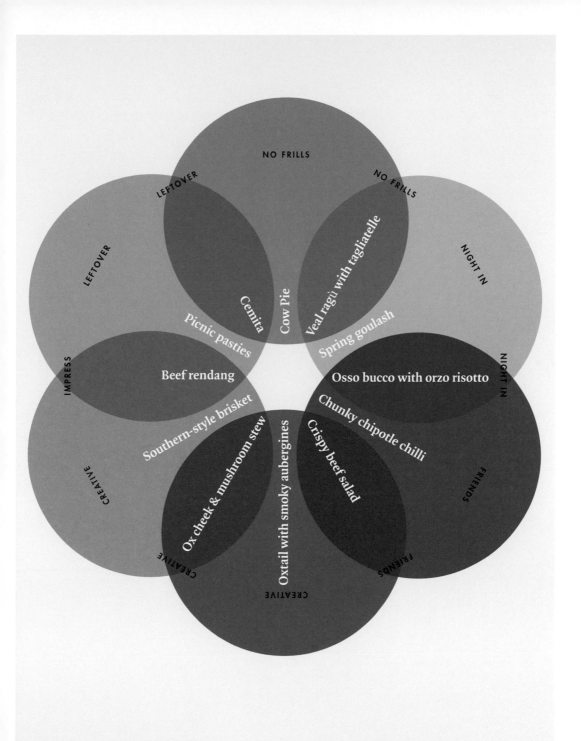

NO FRILLS

NO FRILLS

LEFTOVER

LEFTOVER

NIGHT IN

NIGHT IN

IMPRESS

Cemita

Cow Pie

Veal ragù with tagliatelle

Picnic pasties

Spring goulash

Beef rendang

Osso bucco with orzo risotto

Southern-style brisket

Chunky chipotle chilli

CREATIVE

Crispy beef salad

Ox cheek & mushroom stew

Oxtail with smoky aubergines

FRIENDS

CREATIVE

FRIENDS

CREATIVE

CORE

Braised Beef

Braised Beef

There's nothing difficult about slow-braising a cut of beef – or any other meat for that matter. The joy of it is in the idea that, as you sit back being warmed by the oven, all the hard work is being done for you. Braised beef is tender and juicy. The liquid packs moisture into tough cuts and gently simmers them apart – the longer you braise the better (7 hours is optimum time for faint-worthily tender beef, but as most of us don't have that luxury, 3 hours gets it tender enough to pull). Buy one whole cut of beef, rather than ready-diced – that way you can cut it exactly how you like, or leave it whole and shred it later. You can do all these recipes on the hob too.

Beef loves: thyme, chilli, red wine, white wine, sugar, spice, mushrooms.

Tips for slow cooking

- Marinating tough cuts of beef is never a bad thing and, if you have time, I'd recommend doing it before each of these recipes to get the best flavour and texture out of the meat. A simple marinade can be olive oil, garlic, fresh thyme and chilli – but go with what you fancy.

- Browning the beef first caramelises it, leaving wonderful sticky bits in the bottom of the pan, and adds to the flavour of your dish. You need space in the pan to crisp, so fry the beef in batches if necessary. Turn it when it is dark golden and comes away easily from the bottom of the pan.

- Season the meat just before you fry it or season it 24 hours ahead and leave it in the fridge (this way the moisture will seep out, soak up the salt, then be reabsorbed right through the beef) – anywhere in between and the salt will dry out the moisture, making the beef tough. Adjust the seasoning at the end of cooking.

- Don't boil the meat too vigorously. You want it to cook slow and low. Make it the day ahead – it tastes even better warmed up the next day.

- Make sure your ovenproof dish has a well-fitting lid, or cover it tightly with baking parchment and foil so the braising juices don't evaporate. You can simmer the juices down once the beef is tender.

Best cuts of beef for braising

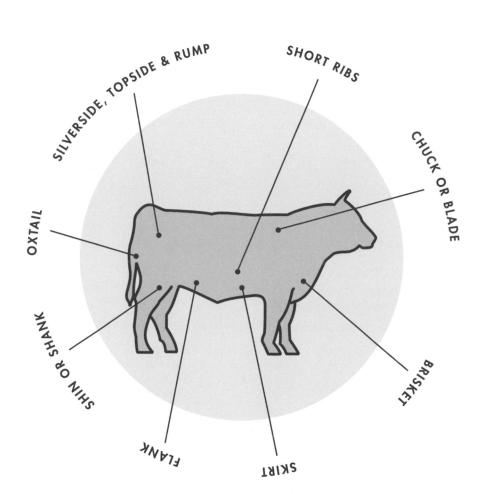

SILVERSIDE, TOPSIDE & RUMP

SHORT RIBS

CHUCK OR BLADE

OXTAIL

SHIN OR SHANK

BRISKET

FLANK

SKIRT

SHORT RIBS

Ribs, gently and slowly braised in beer, bourbon, wine or cider and braised with herbs and spices, loosen up, becoming delicious and tender to nibble from the bone.

CHUCK or BLADE

A dark, large cut from the shoulder blade, ideal for slow cooking. It's often sold as braising steak. Leave whole or dice for casseroling.

BRISKET

A boneless, fatty, cartilaginous belly-cut. Roll it, bind it and braise it whole to slice. It needs long, slow cooking – it can be tough if not left to cook for long enough – but it is fantastic marinated and braised and served with punchy sauces.

SKIRT

Delicious in flavour. Boneless belly cut – next door to brisket. Marinate the day before and use in pasties and pies.

FLANK

Between the rib and the hip (situated between brisket and topside). It's often a steak cut which is quickly seared to keep it tender. Braising helps to tenderise this tough cut.

SILVERSIDE, TOPSIDE AND RUMP

I once had it roasted and it was lacking moisture and was very tough. It's ideally suited to braising or pot-roasting.

SHIN or SHANK

The toughest muscle on the cow – strolling along all day and holding all that weight – therefore the cheapest cut to buy. It is marbled with gelatinous membrane which melts as its cooks, adding flavour and shine to sauces.

OXTAIL

Buy oxtail still on the bone. The marrow, cartilage and fattiness help to produce a stonkingly good flavour. No need for squeamishness – once the meat is pulled off the bone, the texture is just like any other tender beef.

Braised beef

CORE

Knowing how to braise, and realising how simple and delicious it is to do, solves many a kitchen dilemma. It is a brilliant dish to make ahead – no need to fret about last-minute cooking – and it's even tastier warmed up the next day. It's an easy freezer; it works with most store-cupboard ingredients; and you can just leave it in the oven to phut away for a whole day without thinking about it. Sometimes my husband cooks a whole shin overnight at a low temperature to use the next day. You wake up very hungry (and smelling a little roasty) but it comes out of the oven perfectly cooked. Try this core recipe with legs and shoulders of pork, boar, lamb, mutton, hogget. It works just the same. Wrap it in a tortilla, eat it from a bowl, scoff it in a bun, or package it neatly in pastry. The possibilities are endless.

1 tablespoon extra virgin olive oil

1kg good-quality braising beef (see best cuts for braising, page 123)

2 slices unsmoked streaky bacon, finely chopped (optional)

2 banana shallots, finely chopped

2 carrots, peeled and finely chopped

1 stick of celery, finely chopped

175ml white wine

1 bay leaf

1 sprig of fresh thyme

1 x 400g tin of chopped tomatoes

500ml chicken or beef stock

SERVES	TIME TO PREPARE	TIME TO COOK
4–6	20 MINUTES	3–7 HOURS

1. Preheat the oven to 150°C/fan 130°C/gas 1. Heat the oil in a heavy-based ovenproof pan over a high heat. Place the beef in the pan, season lightly, and brown the meat on each side until dark and almost crisp. Remove from the pan and set aside on a plate, loosely covered with foil. Do this in batches if necessary.

2. Turn down the heat slightly and fry the bacon (if using) for 5 minutes in the beef pan until the fat is crisp. Add the chopped shallots, carrots and celery and gently fry for 10–15 minutes, covered, until soft and melting.

3. Put the beef back into the pan to sit on top of the sautéed vegetables. Pour over the wine and bubble for a few minutes to evaporate the alcohol. Add the herbs, chopped tomatoes and stock. Bring to the boil then turn down the heat to a slow simmer. Cover tightly with a lid or parchment and foil, then slide into the oven or keep over a low heat on the hob and cook gently for at least 3 hours, until the meat can be easily pulled apart with two forks.

4. Remove from the oven and slide off the lid. Simmer for another 30 minutes over a medium heat on the hob, to reduce the juices. Serve with mashed potato, as a sauce for pasta, or with some fresh spring greens.

Cow pie

Desperate Dan may not have put porter in his pie, but in this the booze gives depth to the sauce and an explosion of sweet, salty and sharp. Taste the porter before you pour – some can be too bitter and will overwhelm the other flavours in the pie. You want to end up with a glossy, beery roux with fork-tender beef and a crispy pastry top. Next time add shelled oysters, creamy chestnuts or buttery mushrooms.

1 tablespoon olive oil

1kg good-quality beef shin, or skirt steak, cut into 2cm chunks, patted dry and dredged in 1 tablespoon plain flour

3 medium red onions, peeled and quartered

3 cloves of garlic, roughly chopped

1 carrot, peeled and roughly chopped

2 sticks of celery, trimmed and finely chopped

a few sprigs of fresh rosemary, leaves picked and chopped

leaves from a small bunch of fresh thyme

200ml porter or stout (or something lighter if you prefer – red wine will also do)

300ml beef or chicken stock

2 tablespoons Dijon mustard

200g all-butter puff pastry, from a block

1 large free-range egg, beaten

SERVES

4–6

TIME TO PREPARE

25 MINUTES

TIME TO COOK

4–7 HOURS

1. Preheat the oven to 150°C/fan 130°C/gas 1. In a heavy-based, ovenproof pan, heat the oil over a medium-high heat. Add the floured beef (shaking off the excess as it goes into the pan), season lightly, and brown on all sides (about 10 minutes), until beginning to caramelise (you may need to do this in batches). Remove from the pan and set aside on a plate, covered loosely with foil.

2. Put the onions, garlic, carrot and celery into the same pan and cook gently until soft and melting. Season generously.

3. Return the beef to the pan with the vegetables. Add the herbs and pour over the porter and stock. Bring to the boil, then turn down the heat to a slow simmer. Cover the pan tightly with a lid or parchment and foil, then transfer to the oven or keep over a low heat on the hob and cook gently for at least 3 hours, until the meat can be easily pulled apart with two forks.

4. Remove the lid and simmer for another 30 minutes over a medium heat on the hob to reduce the juices. Stir in the mustard, season to taste, then transfer the beef into a 2 litre ovenproof dish and set aside to cool. (This can be made up to 3 days in advance or kept in the freezer for up to 3 months.)

5. Turn the oven temperature up to 200°C/fan 180°C/gas 6. Roll out the pastry on a lightly floured surface to the thickness of a £1 coin. Trim the pastry to fit the top of your ovenproof dish and leave a slight overhang, so it has a chance to shrink. Line the edges of the pie dish with leftover pastry, then brush with beaten egg, so the crust has a platform to lift it from the filling. Punch a small round hole in the centre of the pastry top, then, using a rolling pin to lift it, place it on top of the ovenproof dish. Press the edges down with your index finger, crimping as you go. Brush the top with beaten egg and, using any excess pastry, cut out 2 horns for the top of your pie – brush these with egg too. Slide the pie into the oven and cook for 25–30 minutes, until the pastry is golden, flaky and crisp. Serve with extra mustard and wilted greens.

Veal ragù with tagliatelle

NO FRILLS

A quick note about British rose veal: the raising of rose veal is supported by the UK RSPCA's Freedom Food programme – it's no longer on the blacklist. Calves from dairy cows are now raised on protein-rich diets on farms in the UK and are slaughtered as young beef (not day-old calves). Its pale pink, succulent and tender meat (which used to be white and milky) comes from being well raised and properly looked after. And it is absolutely delicious. Just make sure it's 'rose'.

Slow cooked rose veal – either shin or osso bucco – makes a wonderful ragù for pasta. It's light and flavoursome and breaks down well to use as a sauce. Reduce the juices enough so that they just hold to the pasta and but not so much that you can't mop up the bottom of the plate afterwards. The veal should barely have any bite – you want to know it's

there, but it has to be slurpable. To double this quantity, keep to 1 tin of chopped tomatoes and just a little more stock. And to pinch down to serving 2, halve the quantities exactly.

1 tablespoon extra virgin olive oil
1kg good-quality rose veal shin or 6 cuts of
    rose veal osso bucco
2 slices unsmoked streaky bacon, finely chopped
2 banana shallots, finely chopped
2 carrots, peeled and finely chopped
1 stick of celery, finely chopped
a pinch of freshly grated nutmeg
1 bay leaf
1 sprig of fresh thyme
175ml white wine
1 x 400g tin of chopped tomatoes
1 tablespoon tomato purée
500ml chicken or beef stock
100ml double cream
400g good tagliatelle (fettucine is good too)
Parmesan cheese, grated, to serve

SERVES	TIME TO PREPARE	TIME TO COOK
4–6	15 MINUTES	3–7 HOURS

1. Preheat the oven to 150°C/fan 130°C/gas 1. Heat the oil in a heavy-based ovenproof pan over a medium heat. Season the veal and add it to the pan. Fry the meat, turning it so it browns on all sides, until golden. Remove the veal from the pan and set aside on a plate loosely covered with foil.

2. Fry the bacon in the same pan for 5 minutes, until crisp. Add the chopped shallots, carrots, celery and nutmeg, season well, then cover and gently fry for 10 minutes until softened.

3. Place the veal back in the pan to sit on top of the sautéed vegetables. Add the herbs, then turn up the heat and pour over the wine. Allow to simmer for a few minutes until the alcohol has evaporated, then add the chopped tomatoes, purée and stock. Season generously. Bring to the boil, then turn down the heat to a slow simmer. Cover, then slide into the oven or keep on the hob on a low heat and cook gently for at least 3 hours until the meat can be easily pulled apart with two forks.

4. Remove the lid, add the cream and simmer on the hob for another 30 minutes to reduce the juices. (Once cooled, this can stay in an airtight container in the fridge for up to 4 days, or in the freezer for up to 3 months.)

5. When you are almost ready to serve, bring a pan of salted water to the boil and add the tagliatelle. Cook for 8 minutes, until *al dente*, or according to the packet instructions. Drain and toss with the veal ragù. Top with grated Parmesan.

Spring goulash

This goulash has all the qualities of Hungarian herdsmen – gruff, hearty and cheerful. Adding charred spring onions and wilted spinach makes it a lighter dish for milder days but still makes space for big flavours. If it's the true gulyás you're after, leave the spring veggies out. Make this with veal, pork or lamb instead of beef, following the same method. There is no other way to eat this but from a bowl with a spoon and a big hunk of bread (preferably slurping it through your beard on the side of a mountain).

3 tablespoons olive oil

400g braising steak, chunkily diced

1 onion, finely chopped

1 carrot, peeled and finely chopped

2 teaspoons caraway seeds

2 cloves of garlic, crushed

2 tablespoons sweet paprika, plus extra to serve

a pinch of smoked paprika

3 Jersey Royal new potatoes, quartered

500ml good-quality beef stock, heated

1 x 400g tin of chopped tomatoes

2 roasted red peppers, peeled and chopped (these can be from a jar, rinsed)

200g green beans

2 spring onions, rubbed with olive oil and seasoned

200g spinach, washed thoroughly

soured cream, to serve

SERVES	TIME TO PREPARE	TIME TO COOK
2 GENEROUSLY	**15** MINUTES	**3–7** HOURS

1. Preheat the oven to 150°C/fan 130°C/gas 1. Heat a tablespoon of the olive oil in an ovenproof pan over a medium heat and add the beef. Fry until browned on all sides, then remove from the pan and set aside on a plate, covered with foil.

2. Turn down the heat slightly, and heat the remaining olive oil in the pan. Add the onion, carrot and caraway seeds, season and gently fry, covered, for 10–15 minutes until softened. Stir through the garlic and the paprikas and fry for another minute. Add the potatoes and coat in the spiced vegetables.

3. Pour in the stock, chopped tomatoes and red peppers, then season well with salt and pepper. Bring to the boil and turn to a low simmer. Cover and slide into the oven or keep over a low heat on the hob, then cook, slowly, for at least 3 hours, or until the meat is soft and falling apart and the juices are still soupy. Remove from the oven and set aside on a plate, loosely covered with foil.

4. Bring a pan of salted water to the boil and simmer the green beans for 2 minutes, until just tender. Drain and refresh under cold water. Stir them through the goulash.

5. Heat a griddle pan over a high heat and, when smoking, add the spring onions. Fry for 5 minutes until blackened, then thickly slice. Divide the spinach between two deep bowls and top with the goulash – the spinach will immediately wilt as you pour over the hot beef. Top with the sliced spring onions and serve with a generous dollop of soured cream.

Osso bucco with orzo risotto and gremolata

NIGHT IN

This dish harks back to gluttonous nights in Bolognese trattorie, scoffing down rich risotto and shanks of veal and tossing it all down with sleepy red wine … The Italians sure know how to nail slow cooking.

As the meat cooks, slowly and gently, the bone marrow melts into the sauce and gives it a thick, glossy richness. Cooking the meat this way and at this speed makes it tender enough to pull away at and serve alongside this scrumptious saffron orzo risotto. Orzo is a little oval-shaped pasta – it makes a fabulously soft and creamy risotto and takes little time to cook. You can find rose veal or oxtail in most good butchers, and they're creeping into supermarkets too. This is a more hands-on night in than usual, but so worth it. Just something a little different.

2 tablespoons olive oil
2 x 150g British rose veal shanks or oxtail, dusted in 1 tablespoon plain flour
1 onion, finely chopped
1 carrot, peeled and finely chopped
3 cloves of garlic, crushed
1 bay leaf
leaves from 2 sprigs of fresh oregano
4 juniper berries
500ml passata
50ml red wine
50ml beef stock

FOR THE ORZO RISOTTO
30g unsalted butter
½ an onion, very finely chopped
½ a stick of celery, very finely chopped
a pinch of freshly grated nutmeg
2 cloves of garlic, finely chopped
120g orzo pasta (you can use risotto rice here too, but I love the creamy texture of the pasta)
a splash of white wine or vermouth
400ml fresh chicken or vegetable stock, simmered and left to infuse with a good pinch of saffron (optional)
50g Parmesan cheese, grated

SERVES	TIME TO PREPARE	TIME TO COOK
2	20 MINUTES	3 HOURS

2 tablespoons finely chopped fresh parsley leaves
grated zest of ½ a lemon
1 clove of garlic, crushed

1. Preheat the oven to 150°C/fan 130°C/gas 1. Heat a tablespoon of the olive oil in a large, heavy-based ovenproof saucepan over a medium-high heat and brown the shanks for 4 minutes on each side, until crisp and golden. Remove from the pan and set aside on a plate, loosely covered with foil. Using the same pan, over a slightly lower heat, add another tablespoon of the olive oil and add the onion, carrot and garlic. Season, cover and gently fry for 10–15 minutes until softened.

2. Stir in the bay leaf, oregano and juniper and return the veal shanks to the pan. Pour in the passata, red wine and hot stock, season and bring to the boil. Turn to a low simmer and cover, then slide into the oven or keep over a low heat on the hob and cook for at least 3 hours, until tender. Remove from the oven and place on the hob over a low heat, uncovered, while you make the risotto. (You can make this up to 3 days in advance or freeze it for up to 3 months.)

3. For the orzo, heat 25g of the butter in a large saucepan over a medium-low heat and add the onion, celery and nutmeg. Season, cover and gently fry for 10–15 minutes, until softened. Add the garlic and stir in, frying for 1 minute.

4. Add the orzo and fry for 3 minutes until slightly translucent. Turn up the heat and add the wine, simmering for 2 minutes until the alcohol has evaporated and the liquid is absorbed.

5. Pour a little stock into the pasta and stir until it has absorbed all the liquid. You should be able to see the bottom of the pan here. Repeat this process, adding a little splash of stock at a time, until the pasta is soft. The pasta should have a small bite to it and the sauce should be silky and soupy. Use more stock or water if the pasta needs more cooking.

6. Take the veal off the heat and allow it to rest for 10 minutes, covered loosely with foil. Mix all the ingredients for the gremolata. Season and set aside until ready to serve. Once the pasta is cooked, stir in the remaining butter and the Parmesan and allow it to sit for a few minutes. Season well, and serve immediately in shallow bowls. Top with the braised veal shanks, spooning over the sauce, and garnish with the gremolata.

Chunky chipotle chilli

Bitter chocolate, sweet muscovado and smoky chipotle seep into the meat as it slowly breaks down, giving you just the kick and depth of flavour you need from a spicy chilli. Serve it straight from a big pot at the table, accompanied by small bowls of extra chillies, avocado, soured cream and quartered limes to lighten and lift. Oh, and don't forget the margaritas.

2 tablespoons olive oil

1.5kg beef shin or chuck steak, diced

1 onion, finely chopped

1 stick of celery, finely chopped

1 teaspoon cumin seeds

2–4 thumb-sized chipotle chillies and, for extra heat, a good pinch of dried chilli flakes (check for hotness; some are tasteless, some will blow your head off)

2 bay leaves

2 tablespoons grated 100% cocoa solids dark chocolate

2 x 400g tins of chopped tomatoes

700ml fresh beef stock

1 tablespoon dark muscovado sugar

2 x 400g tins of red kidney beans, drained and well rinsed

450g long-grain rice, rinsed

TO SERVE

chopped fresh coriander leaves

5 limes, quartered

2 red or green chillies, sliced

soured cream

guacamole

SERVES	TIME TO PREPARE	TIME TO COOK
8–10	15 MINUTES	3–7 HOURS

1. Preheat the oven to 150°C/fan 130°C/gas 1. Heat 1 tablespoon of the olive oil in a large ovenproof casserole over a medium-high heat. Add the beef, season, and brown on all sides. Remove the beef from the pan and set aside on a plate, covered with foil.

2. Add the remaining oil to the pan and turn down the heat slightly. Add the onion, celery, cumin, chipotles, chilli flakes and bay leaves, season, then cover and gently fry for 10 minutes until soft and fragrant. Stir in the chocolate, then add the tomatoes, stock and muscovado sugar. Bring to the boil, then turn down the heat to a simmer. Cover tightly with a well-fitting lid or foil and slide into the oven to cook slowly for at least 3 hours, until the meat is soft and falling apart.

3. Remove from the oven, slide off the lid and cook for another 30 minutes on the hob over a medium heat. Then roughly shred the meat, using two forks. Stir in the kidney beans and season to taste.

4. Pour the rice and 540ml water (the best ratio I've worked to is 1 part rice to 1.2 parts water) into a pan with a lid and bring to the boil. Cover tightly with a well-fitting lid or foil. Keep over a very low heat for 20 minutes, or remove from the heat without taking off the lid and leave covered for 25–30 minutes, until the rice is cooked and all the liquid has been absorbed. Remove the lid, fluff up the rice with a fork and tip on to a warm serving platter. Top with freshly chopped coriander. Dish up the chilli at the table, straight from the casserole, serve with the rice, squeeze over the lime wedges, scatter over the fresh chillies and dollop over plenty of soured cream and guacamole.

Crispy beef salad

I'm often left with a few spoonfuls of beef that need finishing up from the day before. This fills me with great excitement (it's almost worth holding some back). No more slow-cooking needed, but a quick flash in the pan with sweet Shaoxing rice wine and sharp lemon zest. Fry the beef to caramelise it – get it golden and almost crisp and serve it with fresh, peppery leaves.

1 clove of garlic

1 red onion, very finely sliced

grated zest and juice of 1 lemon

1 tablespoon olive oil

a knob of unsalted butter

200g braised beef, shredded

200g purple sprouting broccoli, trimmed of
    woody ends

200g rocket

a handful of fresh basil leaves, to serve (optional)

FOR THE DRESSING

1 tablespoon Shaoxing rice wine

½ teaspoon Dijon mustard

½ teaspoon dark brown sugar

4 tablespoons extra virgin olive oil

4 excellent dressings to shake in a jar:

SPICY CIDER VINEGAR & HONEY

1 teaspoon of cider vinegar, a squeeze of honey, 1 small crushed clove of garlic, a few drops of Tabasco, 4 teaspoons of extra virgin olive oil.

SHERRY VINEGAR & MAPLE

1 teaspoon of maple sauce, ½ teaspoon of wholegrain mustard, 1 teaspoon of sherry vinegar, 3 tablespoons of walnut oil.

LIME & MISO

1 teaspoon of fish sauce, 1 teaspoon of rice wine vinegar, 1 teaspoon of white miso, juice of 1 lime and 3 teaspoons of sesame oil. Top with sesame seeds and fresh coriander.

AVOCADO, LEMON & CHILLI

1 mashed ripe avocado, 1 teaspoon of Dijon mustard, 2 tablespoons of fresh lemon juice, ¼ of a fresh red chilli, 2 tablespoons of extra virgin olive oil.

1. Finely chop the garlic and mix in a bowl with the red onion. Toss with the lemon zest and juice and set aside for 20 minutes to macerate. The acid will turn the onions a bright pink.

2. Meanwhile, heat a pan over a medium heat with the olive oil, the butter and the beef. Fry for 5–10 minutes, until beginning to crisp and caramelise, scraping up any bits that have stuck to the bottom of the pan. Set aside, turning off the heat, and cover with foil.

3. Bring a pan of salted water to the boil and add the broccoli. Cook for 4–5 minutes, until tender and bright green. Drain in a colander, then refresh under ice-cold water to stop the cooking. Leave to drip off any excess water, then toss with the onion.

4. Mix together the rice wine, Dijon mustard and sugar until dissolved, then add the 4 tablespoons of olive oil and season to taste. Pour in a little of the lemon juice from the onions, to taste, and whisk until the dressing has emulsified.

5. Toss the rocket in a large bowl with a little of the dressing, then add the broccoli and onions. Top with the crispy beef and drizzle over the rest of the dressing, or to taste. Season, and top with the basil leaves to serve, if you like.

SERVES

4

READY IN

30 MINUTES

BRAISED BEEF

Oxtail with smoky aubergines and boozed tomatoes

Slow cooking – which is the only way to go with oxtail – makes us think of colder months and rich stews, but it doesn't have to always be this way. Marinate your oxtail (this is a good step for all braising if you have time) and gently cook it with spices and shallots the night before, then shred it, warm it in a roasting tin in the oven or over a barbecue, toss it with the herbs and serve it alongside these creamy charred aubergines and boozy tomatoes.

SERVES	TIME TO PREPARE	TIME TO COOK
4–6	30 MINUTES + MARINATING	3 HOURS 30 MINS

1kg oxtail, sliced

4 tablespoons olive oil

2 tablespoons ras el hanout (see page 111)

a bunch of fresh thyme

a good squeeze of honey

a pinch of dried chilli flakes

3 banana shallots, peeled (see tip on page 106) and
    left whole

2 sticks of celery, roughly chopped

5 whole allspice berries

100ml red wine

600ml beef stock

2 bay leaves

2 tablespoons chopped fresh marjoram/oregano

2 tablespoons chopped fresh mint

2 tablespoons chopped fresh coriander

a handful of pitted green olives, halved, to serve
    (optional)

FOR THE AUBERGINES

2 plump, firm aubergines

4 tablespoons olive oil

1 teaspoon dried chilli flakes

leaves from 2 sprigs of fresh rosemary,
    finely chopped

3 baby preserved lemons, scooped of their
    fleshy middles and sliced

FOR THE TOMATOES

400g heirloom tomatoes or a mixed bag
    of baby plum, cherry and beef tomatoes,
    chopped and sliced

175ml dry white wine or sherry

60ml white wine vinegar

2 tablespoons caster sugar

2 teaspoons grated lemon zest

3 teaspoons flaked sea salt

2 tablespoons chopped fresh rosemary leaves

extra virgin olive oil, to drizzle

1. Marinate the oxtail with 2 tablespoons of the olive oil, the ras el hanout, thyme, honey and chilli flakes for at least an hour or overnight in the fridge – bring to room temperature before cooking.

2. Toss the tomatoes with the wine or sherry, vinegar, sugar, lemon zest, salt and rosemary and leave to marinate for at least an hour and up to 2 days.

3. Preheat the oven to 150°C/fan 130°C/gas 1. Heat the remaining 2 tablespoons of olive oil in a large saucepan over a high heat and fry the oxtail until browned all over. This may need to be done in batches. Remove from the pan and set aside.

4. Add a little more olive oil to the pan if necessary, along with the whole shallots, celery and allspice. Season, cover and gently fry for 10 minutes.

5. Pour in the wine and simmer for 2 minutes to evaporate the alcohol. Add the stock and bay leaves and bring to the boil. Transfer to the oven, or keep over a low heat on the hob, and cook for at least 3 hours, until the meat is easily pulled apart with two forks. Leave to cool, then remove the oxtail pieces from the pan with a slotted spoon – the braising juices will be clear and flavoursome, so save them for stocks or to drizzle over the meat. Shred the meat off the tail bone and set aside to cool until ready to serve.

6. Slash the aubergines four times lengthways, leaving the stalk on. Douse them with olive oil, chilli flakes and rosemary and set aside to marinate for at least an hour. Grill or barbecue them for 10 minutes on each side, until charred and completely soft and gooey in the middle, then season well and toss with the preserved lemons.

7. Toss the oxtail with the herbs, olives (if using) and seasoning and serve alongside the shredded aubergines and the tomato salad, drizzled with extra virgin olive oil.

Ox cheek, mushroom and tarragon stew

The seam of fat running through the middle of an ox cheek makes it a delicious thing to slow-cook. Succulent and slurpable, in fact. Serve with creamy mash and a dollop of crème fraîche.

4 large ox cheeks (800g), trimmed of fat, seasoned and rubbed with olive oil
30g unsalted butter
4 rashers of smoked streaky bacon or a 50g piece of pancetta, chunkily chopped
2 large leeks, cut into rounds
200g mixture of chestnut and wild mushrooms
a handful of fresh tarragon leaves, roughly chopped
300ml dry cider
200ml chicken stock
2 bay leaves

1. Place an ovenproof casserole pan over a medium-high heat and add the ox cheeks. Brown the cheeks on all sides, until golden. Remove, set aside on a plate and cover with foil.

2. Add the butter and bacon or pancetta to the casserole, turn down the heat slightly and fry until the bacon is crisp. Add the leeks and mushrooms and gently fry, covered, for 10 minutes. Add most of the tarragon and return the cheeks to the pan.

3. Pour over the cider and simmer for 2 minutes to burn off the alcohol. Add the chicken stock and bring to the boil, then lower to a simmer. Add the bay leaves and slide into the oven to cook for at least 3 hours. After this time, test the tenderness of the cheeks by pulling at them with two forks. They should be easy to shred. If so, begin to pull each cheek into smaller pieces. Season to taste, then stir in the rest of the tarragon. Serve with fluffy garlic mashed potato.

SERVES	TIME TO PREPARE	TIME TO COOK
4	15 MINUTES	3–7 HOURS

Southern-style brisket with Boston beans and slaw

GET CREATIVE

Attentions have turned to American-style barbecue food of late and I can't see a way back from it – it's so good. The beef is rubbed with sweet honey and warming spices and cooked in sticky bourbon to make the most deliciously flavoured meat. Boston beans are naughtily rich and make a great addition to the succulent brisket. Lighten up with the crunchy slaw and bunches of fresh coriander to garnish.

1 teaspoon hot chilli powder

1 tablespoon English mustard powder

1 teaspoon hot smoked paprika

1 teaspoon ground cumin

1 tablespoon ground black pepper

1 teaspoon celery salt

1 tablespoon honey

1 tablespoon olive oil, plus extra for frying

2.5kg beef brisket, with a good amount of fat, lightly scored

1 litre beef or chicken stock

300ml bourbon (real ale will do as well)

1 carrot, peeled and roughly chopped

1 onion, roughly chopped

2 sticks of celery, roughly chopped

1 bay leaf

SERVES	TIME TO PREPARE	TIME TO COOK
8–10	1 HOUR + MARINATING	4½–7 HOURS

FOR THE BOSTON BEANS

500g dried haricot beans

75g molasses sugar

75g dark brown sugar

4 tablespoons made English mustard

¼ teaspoon ground cloves

750ml hot water

1 x 500g piece of smoked pancetta, cut into
    2.5cm pieces

1 medium onion, roughly chopped

FOR THE SLAW

1 red cabbage, very thinly sliced

½ a white cabbage, very thinly sliced

juice of 3 limes

50ml olive oil

a large bunch of fresh coriander, leaves roughly
    chopped (you can experiment with mint, basil
    and parsley here too)

1. Mix the chilli powder, mustard powder, paprika, cumin, black pepper, celery salt, honey and olive oil together and massage into the beef. Leave to marinate for at least 2 hours or overnight in the fridge. Place the beans in a large pot and cover with water by 5cm. Soak overnight and drain. Alternatively, bring a pot with the beans covered with water to the boil, remove from the heat and leave to soak for an hour, then drain.

2. Preheat the oven to 150°C/fan 130°C/gas 1. Heat a little oil in a large roasting tray over a medium-high heat on the hob. Add the beef and brown on all sides. Add the stock and the bourbon or beer, with the vegetables and bay leaf. Bring to the boil, then cover tightly with foil and slide into the oven. Cook for at least 4 hours, basting occasionally, until tender.

3. Meanwhile, prepare the beans. Mix the molasses, brown sugar, mustard and ground cloves with the hot water. Place half the pancetta in a large ovenproof pan with a tight-fitting lid. Layer with half the drained beans. Add the chopped onion in a layer, then top with the remaining beans and pancetta. Pour the molasses mixture over the beans. Bring to a simmer on the hob, then place in the oven with the brisket and cook for the last 3 hours of the beef cooking time, or until the beans are tender. Check after 2 hours and add a little more water or stock if necessary. Season well to taste, and return the beans to the oven. They will have formed a good crust.

4. For the slaw, mix the red and white cabbages together in a large bowl. Squeeze over the lime juice and pour on the olive oil. Season generously and toss with the coriander leaves. Serve alongside the sliced brisket and Boston beans.

Beef rendang

Many of the best suppers are those that use up things that are lurking in your store-cupboard. Pair spices (check them – they could be quite old) with very fresh ginger, chillies and lemongrass, and grind whole seeds where possible – it can be a disappointing dish when you've used chillies that have been left to wrinkle, lemongrass that has dried out, and sad, stringy ginger. Let these ingredients phut away and seep into the beef for a couple of hours and you'll have yourself a magnificent bowlful of food.

2 red onions, roughly chopped
2 sticks lemongrass, peeled of its woody outer layer, or 1 tablespoon lemongrass paste
2 cloves of garlic
2 hot red chillies, roughly chopped
a 5cm piece of fresh root ginger, peeled and grated
2 tablespoons cumin seeds
2 tablespoons coriander seeds
1 teaspoon ground turmeric
1 tablespoon groundnut oil for frying
1kg braising beef (chuck, shin or blade work well here), cut into smaller pieces
2 x 400ml tins of coconut milk
200ml chicken stock
1 tablespoon fish sauce
2 star anise
1 cinnamon stick

SERVES

4–6

TIME TO PREPARE

20 MINUTES

TIME TO COOK

3–7 HOURS

1. Preheat the oven to 150°C/fan 130°C/gas 1. In a food processor or with a hand blender, blend the red onion, lemongrass, garlic, chillies and ginger together until you have a rough paste.

2. Heat a small frying pan over a medium-low heat and add the cumin, coriander and turmeric. Dry-fry the spices for 2 minutes, until fragrant. Remove and grind in a spice grinder or a pestle and mortar.

3. Heat the groundnut oil in a deep frying pan over a medium heat and add the beef. Season and fry for 5 minutes on all sides so it begins to brown (do this in batches if necessary). Remove from the pan, set aside on a plate and cover loosely with foil.

4. Add the paste and ground spices to the beef pan and fry for 2 minutes. Stir the beef back in, then add the remaining ingredients. Cover and place in the oven for at least 3 hours, until the beef is falling apart.

5. Take out of the oven and remove the meat from the pan to a plate. Pull at it roughly with two forks – large bits are good. Put the pan back on a medium-high heat and reduce the liquid by two-thirds to a syrupy sauce, removing the whole spices, then return the shredded meat to the pan. Serve with wilted greens and sticky rice.

Picnic pasties

Too fun not to do, and a scrumptious way to use up leftover beef, or any meat for that matter. Get crimping. Pop them into a basket and head off to the park with a bottl' o' cider.

360g plain flour
¼ teaspoon flaked sea salt
170g cold unsalted butter, cut into cubes
2½ teaspoons ice-cold water
200g leftover braised beef
1 free-range egg, beaten

1. Sift the flour with the sea salt and whiz or rub in and lift the butter with your fingertips until you reach a breadcrumb consistency. Gradually incorporate the ice-cold water (you may not need it all) until the breadcrumbs have moulded into a smooth dough. Cut the dough into 4 equal balls, wrap them in clingfilm and chill in the fridge for 30 minutes. (They can be frozen for up to 3 months too, and defrosted when needed.)

2. Preheat the oven to 200°C/fan 180°C/gas 6. Lightly dust a work surface with flour and remove one ball of dough from the fridge. Using a floured rolling pin, roll it out to a circle the thickness of a £1 coin. Fill one half of the circle with 50g of leftover braised beef, leaving a 2cm rim. Fold the other half of the pastry over and press the edges together, using a little water to bind if necessary. Crimp the edges, pleating, folding and pressing, and lay on a baking tray lined with parchment. Using a fork, poke a few holes in the pastry. Repeat with the remaining dough balls. Brush the finished pasties with the beaten egg.

3. Slide the pasty tray into the oven and bake for 35 minutes, until the pastry is golden and crisp and the beef is heated through. Leave to cool and serve warm, or cool completely and reheat.

SERVES

4

TIME TO PREPARE

10 MINUTES + CHILLING

TIME TO COOK

35 MINUTES

Cemita

This is less a recipe, more an assembly of (delightful) ingredients. Together these morsels (leftover or fresh) build up the most moreish of sandwiches. The cemita (or cemita poblana) is a soft, sweet sesame seed bun stuffed full with smoky chilli and spicy raw onion, soft avocado, crunchy herbs and succulent beef. The true recipe, still produced in a Mexican town called Puebla, uses a lemony mint named papalo, deep fried ground beef or pulled pork carnitas and a mozzarella-like cheese called panela. Now it's my staple for leftovers, and last night's braised beef works a treat. Pile in as many fresh herbs as will fit – they bring so much flavour and freshness.

1 round sesame seed bun (see simple white bread, page 12)
1 ripe avocado, stoned, peeled and sliced
50g leftover braised beef
a few thin slices of mozzarella cheese
1 heaped tablespoon chipotle chilli paste
a few very thin slices of onion
1 plum tomato, thinly sliced crossways
a handful of fresh mint leaves
a large handful of fresh coriander leaves

1. Cut open the buns and layer up all the ingredients. Devour.

MAKES

1 BUN

READY IN

20 MINUTES

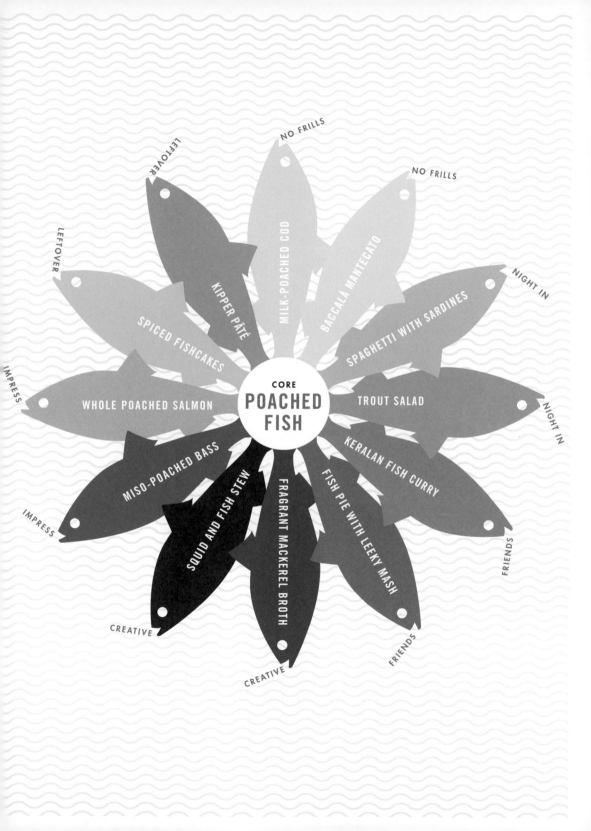

Poached Fish

The delicate nature of fish requires equally gentle cooking. If you buy fresh, well-sourced fish you will need very little to flavour it. Up to 7 minutes' simmering in a pan with a juicy lemon, sliced, buttery shallots, a few peppercorns, a good splash of wine and milk or water will bring out the best in your fish. As it touches the heat the fish will turn from a beautiful raw translucency to a milky, flaking opaqueness. A quick, healthy and delicious way of cooking fish.

The MSC – Marine Stewardship Council – have a reliable fish sustainability chart. Check for updates about which fishies are good to eat and which are best to avoid: www.mcsuk.org.

Fish loves: lemon, parsley, salt, garlic, samphire, chilli, tarragon, chorizo, potatoes, peas.

Fish tips

- When buying fresh fish, check for bright eyes, firm flesh and shiny skin.

- To pin-bone fillets, run a hand over the flesh and, with a pair of tweezers, tug out any bones you come across. To skin, sit the fillet skin-side down, then run a sharp, flat, flexible knife – a bendy filleting knife if you have one – between the skin and the flesh, wiggling the knife along the board to free up the skin. It will come away easily. If buying from a fishmonger's, you can ask them to do it for you. The skin easily peels away after poaching, so if you'd rather not use a knife, or are cooking large fillets or whole fish, remove the skin this way.

- The flaky structure of fish – even large steaks – makes it susceptible to falling apart as it poaches, especially if the skin has been removed. To avoid this, wrap the fish in muslin or cheesecloth and gently tie the ends with string.

Poached fish

A simple technique – light and fragrant – for cooking any fishy, whether smoked, fresh, filleted or whole. Simmer the poaching liquid, don't boil it, and be careful when lifting the fish out of the pan as it flakes easily. Use this quick recipe as a starting point for making pâté, pies and curries and reserve the liquid for stock, or serve the poached fish on its own with crushed new potatoes, sweet, tender vegetables or a herb gremolata.

15g unsalted butter
2 banana shallots, finely sliced
1 small leek or fennel bulb, finely sliced
1 bay leaf
4 black peppercorns
1 clove
2 cloves of garlic, sliced
100ml white wine
50ml fresh fish stock or water
4 x 250g sustainable fish fillets
whole milk or double cream (optional)
1 teaspoon fennel seeds

1. In a large saucepan or deep frying pan, melt the butter over a medium-low heat and add the sliced shallots and leek or fennel with the bay leaf, peppercorns and clove. Season well and gently fry, covered, for 10–15 minutes, until softened. Uncover, add the garlic and fry for 1 minute. Pour over the wine and stock, bring to the boil, then turn down to a gentle simmer.

2. Place the fish fillets in the pan, making sure they are submerged in liquid. Very gently simmer for 5–7 minutes, until the fish is just flaking and opaque. Remove the dish from the oven and spoon the fish on to a plate with a sheet of kitchen paper to soak up extra juices.

3. Bring the poaching juices to the boil and simmer to reduce. If you like, add a little milk or cream to the reduction and pour over the fish or keep as it is for a rich sauce or to make a base for a stew, pie or soup. Season the fish and serve immediately. If turning the fish into a pie or fishcakes, you can poach it the day before and keep it, wrapped up, in the fridge.

SERVES

4

READY IN

20 MINUTES

Milk-poached cod with mushy peas and tartare sauce

NO FRILLS

I was conscious that leaving cod unbattered to eat alongside sweet mushy peas and salty tartare could sound somewhat underwhelming, but the truth is that a well-seasoned, super-fresh bit of fish needs no thick batter to weigh it down, and all it calls for is something fine and untempered to go beside it. Poaching in milk enriches the fish, gives chalky fillets a good shine and produces a flavourful liquor for white sauces. Crushed petits pois – not a marrowfat bean in sight, handsome as they are – with a good lot of butter and mint, and tender new potatoes dunked in tartare, is all this dish needs.

15g unsalted butter
2 banana shallots, finely sliced
1 small leek or fennel bulb, finely sliced
2 cloves of garlic, sliced
1 bay leaf
a bunch of fresh thyme
100ml white wine
50ml whole milk
4 x 250g responsibly caught cod fillets (MSC certified), skinned

FOR THE MUSHY PEAS
400g petits pois
30g unsalted butter, melted
a handful of fresh mint leaves

FOR THE TARTARE SAUCE
1 tablespoon capers, drained and chopped
8 cornichons, chopped
2 tablespoons finely chopped fresh tarragon
2 tablespoons good-quality mayonnaise
4 tablespoons natural yoghurt
a drop of Tabasco
juice of ½ a lemon, plus extra wedges to serve

SERVES

4

READY IN

30 MINUTES

1. First, make the mushy peas. Blanch the peas in a pan of boiling water for 3 minutes, or until tender, then drain well. Place them in a food processor and blitz with the butter and mint leaves. Place in a clean saucepan ready to warm.

2. Mix all the ingredients for the tartare sauce in a bowl and season to taste. Set aside at room temperature, or keep in the fridge if serving later. (You can make the peas and the tartare sauce a day ahead.)

3. Melt the butter in a large saucepan or deep frying pan over a medium heat and add the sliced shallots, leek and garlic along with the herbs. Season, cover and gently fry for 10–15 minutes, until softened. Pour in the wine and boil for 2 minutes to evaporate the alcohol, then turn down the heat to a gentle simmer and add the milk. Bring to the boil, then turn down to a simmer again. Lower in the cod fillets, so that they are completely covered by liquid (if they are peeping out, add more milk or turn halfway through cooking). Simmer very gently for 5–7 minutes, until the fish is flaky and opaque.

4. Meanwhile, warm the pan of mushy peas over a medium heat. Spoon on to warmed plates. Using a fish slice or a slotted spoon, transfer the cod on to the mushy peas. Serve with a dollop of tartare sauce and boiled new potatoes, if you like. Reserve the poaching liquid for fish pie and chowder.

Baccalà mantecato (Creamed salt cod)

NO FRILLS

Salt cod sits quite comfortably within my fixation for things that are preserved, cured, pickled or soused. Though not drenched in vinegar, smoked with hickory or brined with saltpetre, salt cod lasts for a very, very long time – for ever, actually – out of the fridge without turning, which means it's the perfect thing (along with the cornichons and olives) to keep handy in your kitchen and whip out when the pennies are tight.

Salt cod does require a bit of thinking ahead – so plan when you want to eat it. You'll need to soak it for up to 2 days to soften up the fish ready for poaching – it is salted and then dried, so it needs to be well rehydrated and rinsed regularly. Baccalà mantecato is creamy, salty and warming, and a wonderful thing to eat.

400–600g salt cod (avoid fillets with large bones in them, as they may take up half the weight)
15g unsalted butter
4 banana shallots, finely sliced
1 small leek or fennel bulb, finely sliced
100ml dry white wine
1 litre whole milk, or enough to cover the cod
1 bay leaf
4 black peppercorns
1 clove
3 cloves of garlic, crushed
275ml light-flavoured olive oil
extra virgin olive oil, to drizzle
chopped fresh parsley leaves, to serve

SERVES

4 AS A STARTER

TIME TO PREPARE

15 MINUTES + SOAKING

TIME TO COOK

20 MINUTES

1. Put your salt cod into a large basin of water and leave it to soak for 24–48 hours, until tender. Change the water every now and then (this is an essential step, otherwise the fish holds its salty flavour).

2. Melt the butter in a large pan and add the shallots and the leek or fennel. Gently fry over a medium-low heat for 10–15 minutes. Add the wine and simmer until the alcohol has evaporated. Add the soaked and drained cod and pour over the milk with the bay leaf, peppercorns and clove – you should have enough liquid to just cover the fish.

3. Bring to a gentle boil, then lower the heat and simmer for 20 minutes, by which point the cod should start to flake. Try it – if it's still chewy, simmer it for another 5–10 minutes. Take the pan off the heat and transfer the fish to a bowl, using a slotted spoon. Remove and discard any bones. Strain the poaching liquid into a jug and leave the cod to cool a little.

4. In a blender or food processor, whiz the cod with the garlic, seasoning with pepper to taste and salt if it needs it – remember, it will already be salty. Still whizzing, pour a slow stream of olive oil into the cod until it emulsifies and becomes a thick, light and silky paste. Serve still warm or at room temperature, on hunks of toasted bread with a drizzle of extra virgin olive oil and a scattering of chopped parsley.

Sardine, chilli and fennel spaghetti (Pasta con le sarde)

This is one of my favourite dishes for an evening toute seule or à deux. With the level of delight that comes from eating a bowl of this, you may as well be right there on the coast of Sardinia. If you can't get hold of any sardines, or you can't face the bones, go for fresh anchovies, whose bones are too small to notice. Alternatively, leave out the fish altogether and up the fennel.

15g unsalted butter

2 banana shallots, finely sliced

1 fennel bulb, finely shaved, reserving the fronds

1 bay leaf

4 black peppercorns

1 clove

100ml white wine

50ml fish stock

6 fresh sardine fillets, gutted and skinned

a good glug of extra virgin olive oil, plus extra
    for drizzling

2 cloves of garlic

½ teaspoon dried chilli flakes

1 teaspoon fennel seeds

2 tablespoons pine nuts, toasted

1 tablespoon flaked almonds, toasted

2 tablespoons raisins, soaked in water overnight,
    then drained

200g spaghetti

2 tablespoons chopped fresh parsley leaves

a handful of breadcrumbs, toasted, to serve

SERVES	TIME TO PREPARE	TIME TO COOK
2	10 MINUTES	30 MINUTES

1. In a large saucepan, melt the butter over a medium-low heat and add the sliced shallots and half the fennel with the bay leaf, peppercorns and clove. Season well and gently fry for 10–15 minutes, covered, until softened. Pour over the wine, turn up the heat to bubble, then add the stock. Bring to the boil, then turn down the heat to a simmer. Place the sardine fillets on top, making sure they are submerged in the liquid. Very gently simmer for 3–5 minutes, until the sardines are flaky and cooked through. Using a slotted spoon, lift the fish on to a plate. Peel back any skin and pick out any large bones. Strain the contents of the pan and set aside to use as a base for soups.

2. Heat a splosh of olive oil in the fish pan over a gentle heat and add the rest of the fennel. Stir in the garlic, chilli and fennel seeds and fry gently for 3 minutes until the fennel starts to turn golden. Add the pine nuts, almonds and raisins to heat through then set aside. Season well.

3. Meanwhile, bring a pan of salted water to the boil and add the spaghetti. Cook for 8 minutes, or according to the packet instructions, until *al dente*. Drain, reserving 1 tablespoon of the pasta water, then drizzle the spaghetti lightly with olive oil. Toss with the fennel, adding the reserved pasta water. Gently stir in the parsley and the poached sardine fillets and divide between shallow pasta bowls. Drizzle with olive oil and season well to serve. Top with the crispy breadcrumbs.

Trout salad with beetroot and horseradish dressing

Make a parcel around fresh, pink trout fillets with baking parchment, douse them in wine and butter, scatter with herbs, and poach in the oven. This is a different technique to the core recipe but is a good poaching method to keep in reserve in case of hoblessness. It is a more gentle way of poaching, with less liquid, so it needs a little longer in the oven. Sometimes it's just a bonny way of serving the fish, straight from the wrapper. Just lovely.

FOR THE TROUT

15g unsalted butter

2 banana shallots, finely sliced

1 small leek or fennel bulb, finely sliced (75g)

100ml white wine

2 tablespoons chopped fresh thyme leaves

4 black peppercorns

4 tablespoons fish stock

2 x 300g responsibly caught trout fillets, skinned

4 slices of lemon

FOR THE SALAD

15 baby new potatoes

50g watercress, washed and dried

4 cooked and peeled beetroot, cut into matchsticks

50g pea shoots

2 spring onions, sliced on an angle

FOR THE DRESSING

1 tablespoon freshly grated horseradish

juice of ½ a lemon, or to taste

a pinch of sugar

1 teaspoon white wine vinegar

2 tablespoons extra virgin olive oil

2 tablespoons Greek yoghurt

1. Start with the salad. Bring the potatoes to the boil in a medium pan of slightly salted water, then reduce the heat and simmer for 15 minutes, until tender. When pierced with a knife, the potato should slide off easily. Drain and leave the potatoes to cool slightly, then cut into quarters. Set aside.

2. Melt the butter in a saucepan over a medium heat and add the chopped shallots and the leek or fennel. Season well and gently fry for 10–15 minutes, covered, until soft. Add the white wine, thyme and peppercorns. Turn up the heat and simmer the liquid for 2 minutes, until the alcohol has evaporated. Add the fish stock and set aside.

3. Preheat the oven to 180°C/fan 160°C/gas 4. Cut two 40 x 40cm squares of baking parchment and place them flat on a board. Place a trout fillet two-thirds of the way down each square and fold in the edges. Spoon the shallots and the juices over the fish. Lay 2 lemon slices on each fillet, then fold the longer side of the square over the fish. Fold and pleat the edges of the parchment together as though crimping a pasty. You want the parcel to be quite loose, so that the steam from the poaching liquid has space to circulate. When you've made 2 parcels, place them in an ovenproof dish. Slide the dish into the oven and cook for 15 minutes, until the fish is pale pink and opaque.

4. Meanwhile, make the dressing. Mix the grated horseradish with the lemon juice, sugar and white wine vinegar. Whisk in the olive oil until combined and thick, then stir in the yoghurt.

5. Toss the potatoes with the dressing, then stir in the watercress. Place the beetroot on top – without tossing, as this will turn the whole thing purple – and scatter pea shoots on top. Flake over the trout and lightly pour over the dressing. Drizzle with a little extra olive oil and season with salt and pepper, then scatter over the spring onions and serve.

SERVES	TIME TO PREPARE	TIME TO COOK
2–4	15 MINUTES	40 MINUTES

Keralan fish curry

Soft, pure-flavoured white fish is a great partner for spice, as its fresh-tasting, muted tones won't overwhelm the fresh aromatics. You want to develop the flavours of the curry before adding the fish to lightly poach, so season to taste as you go and make sure all your ingredients are fragrant and fresh, and just the heat you like them. With any luck, most of these spices will be loitering in your store-cupboard. Roll limes along the tabletop before you squeeze to get them juicy.

1 teaspoon black mustard seeds

2 tablespoons coconut oil (always have a jar in the cupboard – it's a delicious base for curries and makes a superb hand cream for all you washer-uppers out there; Biona do a good one)

15 fresh curry leaves (available from Natoora or Indian supermarkets; freeze-dried aren't really worth the bother – if you can't find fresh, use a pinch of mild curry powder instead)

1 tablespoon cumin seeds

1 tablespoon garam masala (jarred or fresh, see page 43)

1 teaspoon mild chilli powder

2 teaspoons ground turmeric

2 small onions, finely chopped

½–1 red chilli

a 4cm piece of fresh root ginger, peeled and grated

2 cloves of garlic, finely chopped

1 x 400ml tin of coconut milk

200ml fish stock

500g responsibly caught firm white fish, skin removed, cut into 5cm chunks

juice of 2 limes

2 tablespoons desiccated coconut

TO SERVE
lime wedges
a handful of fresh coriander, chopped
cooked basmati rice

1. Fry the mustard seeds in the coconut oil over a medium heat for 3 minutes, or until the seeds begin to pop. Add the curry leaves and the dry spices and fry for 2 minutes, until fragrant. Add the onions with a drop of water, season and fry for 10 minutes, covered, until softened. Then stir in the fresh chilli, ginger and garlic, frying for another minute.

2. Pour in the coconut milk and stock and bring to the boil. Turn down the heat and simmer for 10 minutes, uncovered, to reduce slightly. Add the fish and poach for 5–7 minutes until cooked through. Squeeze in the lime juice and stir in with the desiccated coconut. Serve in bowls with the chopped coriander, lime wedges and fluffy basmati rice.

SERVES

2

READY IN

40 MINUTES

Fish pie with leeky mash

FEEDING FRIENDS

You can't have a poached fish chapter in a recipe book without a fish pie. It's a great staple for feeding friends – cheap, very cheerful, and the fish goes far – and it's the sort of thing most people love to eat. I put an egg in mine – I think it makes the fish pie – but I know a lot of friends who'd shiver at the thought. Experiment: stir in wilted spinach; add scallops with fresh tarragon; flake in kippers or smoked haddock and top with a cheesy mash.

400ml whole milk

200ml double cream

½ teaspoon freshly grated nutmeg

1 banana shallot, peeled and halved

450g sustainable skinless white fish fillets,
    one type or a mixture

100g raw king prawns, shelled

1 large hard-boiled egg, quartered (optional)

75g unsalted butter

2 tablespoons plain flour

750g floury potatoes, skins left on, cut into
    equal-sized pieces

1 large leek, roughly chopped and rinsed well

20g Parmesan cheese, grated

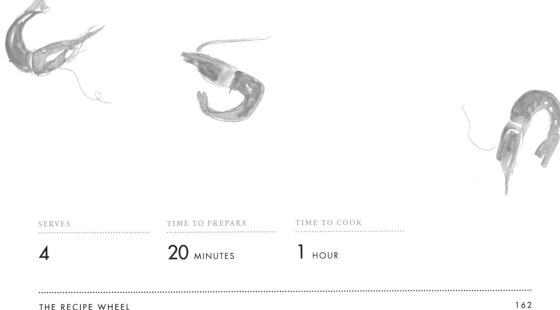

SERVES	TIME TO PREPARE	TIME TO COOK
4	20 MINUTES	1 HOUR

1. Reserving some for the mash, put almost all the milk into a large pan with the cream, nutmeg and shallot and bring to the boil. Add the fish and simmer for 5–7 minutes, until just cooked through. Remove the pan from the heat and add the prawns. When they are pink, remove the fish, prawns and shallots to a plate, using a slotted spoon, and strain the poaching liquid into a jug.

2. When the fish is cool enough to handle, remove any bones and flake into a 1.5 litre shallow ovenproof dish, scattering over the prawns, shallots and egg (if using).

3. Melt 50g of the butter in a pan, add the flour and cook over a medium-low heat, stirring, for 1 minute. Lower the heat right down, then gradually stir in the reserved cooking liquid, adding more as it thickens. Season well and pour over the fish. Leave to cool.

4. Boil the potatoes in a pan of salted water for 20 minutes, or until soft. Meanwhile, melt the remaining 25g of butter in a small pan, add the sliced leek and cook gently for 3–4 minutes, until tender.

5. Drain the potatoes well, then briefly return them to the pan over a low heat to dry. Mash the potatoes until smooth. Stir in the buttery leeks, the Parmesan, and a little of the remaining milk, to make a spreadable but not too wet mash. Season with salt and freshly ground black pepper.

6. Preheat the grill to medium. Spoon the mash over the top of the pie and spread it out in an even layer. Rough up the surface with a fork or the back of a spoon and slide it on the middle shelf under the grill. Grill for 15–20 minutes, until bubbling and golden brown.

Fragrant Asian-style mackerel broth with kohlrabi

Kohlrabi is an unusual member of the brassica family. It resembles the head of a weird little alien, has a bulbous bottom like a turnip, shares the jade green or red purple of larger cabbages, and is crisp in texture like a firm radish. A rare but beautiful edible plant. Its clean crunch and refreshing flavour go very well with salty, flaking mackerel.

Next time, thinly slice kohlrabi and serve with cold poached mackerel for a fresh, crunchy salad.

200g ribbon rice noodles
a splash of rice or white wine vinegar
1 tablespoon groundnut oil, plus extra
  for the noodles
3 shallots, finely sliced
1 red chilli, finely sliced
1 clove of garlic, finely sliced
10 fennel seeds
1.5 litres good-quality fresh fish stock (the stock is
  the base to the broth, so try to find one that
  tastes good)
2 star anise
2 tablespoons fish sauce
1 tablespoon soy sauce
4 fillets of mackerel (300g), skinned and pin-boned
200g kohlrabi, finely cut into matchsticks
chilli oil, to serve

SERVES

4–6

READY IN

30 MINUTES

1. Soak the noodles in just-boiled water with a little vinegar for 15 minutes until tender, or according to packet instructions, then drain and refresh under cold water. Add a little groundnut oil to stop the noodles sticking.

2. Meanwhile, heat the oil in a large saucepan and add the shallots. Season and fry gently for 5 minutes until just soft, then add the chilli, garlic and fennel seeds. Cook for another minute until fragrant. Pour in the fish stock and add the star anise with the fish sauce and soy. Simmer for 8 minutes.

3. Slice each mackerel fillet into 2 pieces and add to the pan, along with the kohlrabi, so the fish is submerged. Poach on a very gentle simmer for 5 minutes.

4. Stir the noodles into the broth to heat, then serve in deep bowls, dividing up the fish and noodles equally. Spoon a little chilli oil on top of the soup and slurp.

Squid and fish stew with rouille

One for hot days or cold snaps. Squid is braised to soften it and pick up all the flavours and warmth of the rich, smoky tomato stew. The fish is then added for the last 5 minutes to poach briefly and keep its freshness. Bread must be at hand to help polish the bowl. This is feel-good, home food.

Keep the rouille for up to 1 week in an airtight jar in the fridge. For a quick version, mix crushed garlic and cayenne into good-quality shop-bought mayonnaise and season to taste before serving.

Next time, mix it up with clams, oysters, crab and salmon. Mussels are a delicious addition too. Steam open fresh, clean mussels in the last 5 minutes of simmering the soup: put the lid on until the shells are fully open, discarding any that are still closed.

1 tablespoon olive oil
2 banana shallots, peeled and finely sliced
1 fennel bulb, trimmed and finely sliced
2 cloves of garlic, sliced
1 tablespoon fennel seeds
1 teaspoon smoked paprika
¼ teaspoon dried chilli flakes
100ml white wine
1 tablespoon tomato purée
1 litre fresh fish stock
1 x 400g tin of chopped tomatoes
200g squid, cleaned, bodies thinly sliced
    and tentacles left whole
800g sustainably caught firm white fish, skinned
    and cut into large chunks
a handful of fresh parsley leaves, chopped, to serve

FOR THE ROUILLE
4 cloves of garlic, crushed
1 large free-range egg yolk
1 teaspoon cayenne pepper
50g fine breadcrumbs
200ml mild olive oil

SERVES

6–8

TIME TO PREPARE

10 MINUTES

TIME TO COOK

1 HOUR

1. Heat the olive oil in a pan over a medium heat and add the shallots and fennel. Season, then cover and gently fry for 10–15 minutes, until softened. Add the garlic and spices and fry for a minute more before turning up the heat and pouring in the white wine. Simmer for a few minutes to evaporate the alcohol.

2. Stir in the tomato purée, fish stock and chopped tomatoes. Bring to the boil, then add the squid and turn the heat to medium-low, to gently simmer for 45 minutes until the squid is tender.

3. Meanwhile make the rouille. Put all the ingredients apart from the olive oil into a large bowl. Whisk until smooth, pale and slightly thickened, then slowly pour in the olive oil, continuously whisking, until the sauce emulsifies and is thick and shiny. Transfer the rouille to a bowl and set aside.

4. When the squid is tender, add the fish to the pan, pushing it gently down into the stew, and gently simmer for another 5–7 minutes, until just cooked through.

5. Ladle into deep bowls, dividing the fish and squid equally, and top with a generous spoonful of the rouille. Sprinkle with parsley, season, and serve with hunks of crusty bread or boiled new potatoes.

Miso-poached bass with warm soba noodle salad

COOK TO IMPRESS

There are moments when all I can think about is noodles – fresh, wholesome and zingily dressed, and, at times, crispy. For a recipe that boasts quite a few fancy ingredients, it has a wonderfully clean and uncomplicated taste. Bass is a deliciously fragrant fish but not too powerful – instead it binds the lime, vinegar and sweet miso flavours together. Whites, blacks, muted browns and vibrant greens are a pleasure to have on the plate.

175g soba noodles
4 tablespoons groundnut oil, plus extra for greasing
20g sweet white miso paste (Clearspring, from Waitrose)
600ml heated fish stock or boiling water
2 teaspoons brown rice vinegar
4 fillets of responsibly sourced sea bass or bream (skin on)
150g enoki or oyster mushrooms
6 spring onions, finely shredded
a small bunch of fresh coriander, chopped
30g pickled ginger
1 teaspoon sesame seeds
1 sheet of nori seaweed, crushed (Clearspring, from Waitrose)

FOR THE DRESSING
50ml brown rice vinegar
1 tablespoon dark brown sugar
1 tablespoon toasted sesame oil
a pinch of dried chilli flakes
grated zest and juice of 1 lime, plus extra wedges to serve

SERVES

4

READY IN

30 MINUTES

1. Bring a pan of lightly salted water to the boil. Add the soba noodles and cook for 5 minutes, or according to the packet instructions, until *al dente*. Drain and rinse under cold water. Set aside in a large serving bowl and toss with a little groundnut oil to keep the noodles from sticking.

2. Heat the remaining groundnut oil in a frying pan and set over a high heat. When the oil starts to shimmer, add a small handful of the cooked noodles and fry for 5 minutes until golden and crisp. Remove the noodles with tongs, leaving the oil in the pan to cool (you can decant the toasted oil and re-use it in salad dressings or stir-fries).

3. Mix the miso paste with the heated fish stock or boiling water, a splash of brown rice vinegar and a pinch of salt in a large pan and set over a medium-high heat. Bring the miso to the boil, then turn down the heat to a simmer. Lower in the sea bass fillets, making sure they are covered by liquid. Gently simmer for 5–7 minutes, until cooked through.

4. Meanwhile, mix the dressing ingredients in a small pan over a low heat and warm until the sugar dissolves. Remove from the heat, then pour the warm dressing over the noodles. Toss with the mushrooms, spring onions, coriander, ginger and sesame seeds. Divide between warm plates.

5. Remove the sea bass from the miso poaching liquid with a fish slice, peel off the skin if you like, and place on top of the noodles. Spoon over a little of the miso broth, season well and top with the crushed seaweed and the crispy noodles. Serve immediately, with cups of the miso on the side and extra lime wedges. Delicious cold too.

Whole poached salmon with lemon and dill

A surprisingly easy and undemanding dish. A side of salmon on a platter is the simplest way to impress a crowd. It takes 30 minutes to make, most of which is taken up by leaving it to rest and gently continue cooking off the heat. You can buy a fish kettle for about £20, but a roasting tray works just as well – bear in mind, though, that you may have to trim or halve your fish to fit the tray. Try this with sea trout next time.

1–1.3kg side of salmon, skinned and pin-boned
(see tips, page 150)
2 bay leaves
a bunch of fresh thyme
1 lemon, sliced, plus extra to serve
fine sea salt (you need 1 tablespoon for every
1.2 litres of water)
a handful of fresh dill leaves, chopped, to serve
aioli, to serve (see page 102)

1. Place the fish in a large roasting tray or fish kettle with the bay leaves, thyme and a few slices of lemon and just cover with salted water (see above). Then, over a medium-high heat, bring the water to the boil. As soon as the water is bubbling, cover tightly with foil and remove from the heat. Set aside and leave to cool – the salmon will continue to cook as the water cools. You want it to be fresh and flaky. No dry squeakiness.

2. Using two fish slices, remove the salmon from the water after 20 minutes and drain on kitchen paper. You can serve the salmon warm, or allow it to cool completely. Move it to a large serving platter and serve, squeezing over lemon juice and seasoning with salt, pepper and the dill leaves, and with a large bowl of aioli alongside, if you like.

SERVES	TIME TO PREPARE	TIME TO COOK
10–15	10 MINUTES + COOLING	15 MINUTES

Spiced fishcakes

Fishcakes are super-quick to produce and extremely cheap if you have most of the ingredients already. They are brilliant for lunch, dinner, canapés, or breakfast if you're that way inclined. Have them on picnics, as a midday snack, or freeze them for another time. Mix sweet chilli with fish sauce and rice wine vinegar to make a dip for dunking the fishcakes. What's not to love?

250g cooked fish
1 teaspoon fish sauce
½ teaspoon grated fresh root ginger
grated zest of 1 lime
2 lime leaves
1 teaspoon granulated sugar
1 tablespoon red curry paste
1 spring onion, sliced
1 tablespoon chopped fresh Thai basil leaves or coriander leaves
2 tablespoons coconut oil or sunflower oil, for frying

1. Put the fish, fish sauce, ginger, lime zest, lime leaves, sugar and curry paste into a food processor and whiz together. Season to taste – you may want to add more ginger, or more fish sauce, or you may need more lime. See how you feel, season to taste, but don't make the mixture too wet or it will be difficult to handle. Stir in the spring onions and herbs.

2. Mould the mixture into 10–12 small, evenly sized patties, place on a plate or tray and chill in the fridge for 15 minutes to firm up. Just before frying, heat the oil in a wide frying pan until shimmering. Add the fishcakes and fry for 2 minutes on each side, until golden and starting to crisp. Serve immediately, or save for tomorrow.

MAKES

READY IN

10–12 FISHCAKES   30 MINUTES

Kipper pâté and pickled cucumber

Dad has a whole kipper every Christmas; a breakfast of meticulous bone-pinching and nit-picking. His favourite thing. While there is something appealing about the smell of smoked fish and going to all that trouble, I'd rather avoid the toil. Making a pâté does just that.

Lightly poaching the kippers (or baking them with butter, which is what he does) softens the fish and makes it easy to remove larger bones, using tweezers. Whizzing it up with yoghurt blends any bones that are fine, hair-like and too small to see. It's a great way to use up leftover fish too.

Serve with the lightly pickled cucumber. It is perfect with any pâté or rillettes, so make more than you need and keep it in an airtight jar for up to a month.

Things to serve with the pâté: cornichons, pickled onions, rye bread, rocket, watercress, poached egg or boiled quail's eggs, pickled shallots, potato cakes, blanched asparagus for dunking.

15g unsalted butter
2 banana shallots, finely sliced
1 small leek or fennel bulb, finely sliced
500ml whole milk
1 bay leaf
4 black peppercorns
1 clove
250g naturally smoked kipper fillets
4 tablespoons Greek yoghurt or crème fraîche
juice of ½ a lemon
1 teaspoon Tabasco
8 slices of brown bread

FOR THE PICKLED CUCUMBER
8 tablespoons white wine vinegar
3 tablespoons caster sugar
6 black peppercorns
1 cucumber, finely sliced or shaved with
    a vegetable peeler
2 tablespoons chopped fresh dill

SERVES	MAKES	READY IN
4	300G	40 MINUTES

1. Melt the butter in a pan and fry the shallots and leek or fennel, covered, for 10–15 minutes, until soft (frying time can be shortened if you like – the smoky flavour will override the shallots – but it gives you a better-tasting broth should you use it later for fish pie). Add the milk, bay leaf and spices and bring to the boil. Turn down to a very gentle simmer. Lower in the smoked kipper fillets, making sure the fish is submerged, then poach for 5–7 minutes, until tender and flaky. Remove with a slotted spoon on to a chopping board and allow to cool slightly. Gently peel away and discard the skin and any large bones.

2. Place the fish in a food processor and whiz with the yoghurt, lemon juice and Tabasco. Season well with black pepper and salt to taste – you may not need to add any extra salt to the kipper. Place in a sterilised airtight jar and keep cool in the fridge until ready to use.

3. For the pickle, place the vinegar and sugar in a small saucepan and set over a medium heat until the sugar dissolves. Add the peppercorns and cucumber and simmer for 5 minutes, until the cucumber is soft and the vinegar has reduced by half. Add the dill and leave to cool completely.

4. Toast the bread briefly, then remove and carefully slice it cleanly through its centre, using a thin serrated knife. Put back into the toaster until you have very thin, crisp Melba toasts. Spread over the kipper pâté and serve with the pickled cucumber.

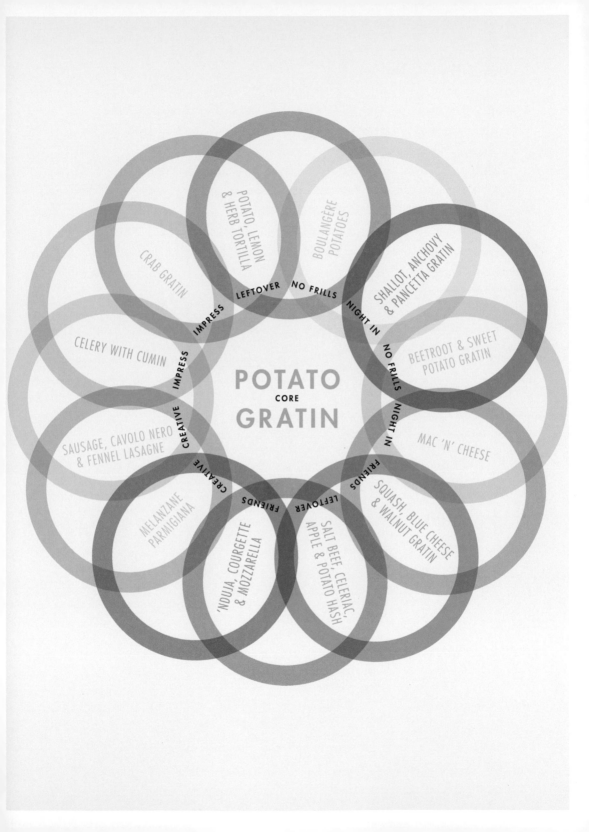

POTATO
CORE
GRATIN

POTATO, LEMON & HERB TORTILLA

BOULANGÈRE POTATOES

SHALLOT, ANCHOVY & PANCETTA GRATIN

CRAB GRATIN

LEFTOVER   NO FRILLS

NIGHT IN

BEETROOT & SWEET POTATO GRATIN

CELERY WITH CUMIN

IMPRESS

IMPRESS

NO FRILLS

NIGHT IN

MAC 'N' CHEESE

SAUSAGE, CAVOLO NERO & FENNEL LASAGNE

CREATIVE

FRIENDS

SQUASH, BLUE CHEESE & WALNUT GRATIN

MELANZANE PARMIGIANA

CREATIVE

FRIENDS   LEFTOVER

SALT BEEF, CELERIAC, APPLE & POTATO HASH

'NDUJA, COURGETTE & MOZZARELLA

Potato Gratin

A gratin is humble peasant food, fit for kings. The name comes from the French word *gratter*, to scrape, or to grate – using up leftover breadcrumbs, nuts or cheese to form a (ridiculously good) crust on top of vegetables or meat. The layers beneath can be built up with what you have to hand – onions, potatoes, fresh thyme, cheese and cream are an unbeatable combination – and seasoned with herbs and salt. Pour over cream or stock that will be absorbed into the base and scatter over a topping.

Serve the gratin as the main event – it doesn't have to be a side dish. It's comfort food. You go back for more, but the second time you miss out the plate and spoon it right into your mouth. It's heaven. Gratins make wonderful leftovers too, and are lovely warmed up the next day with cold ham and a giant tray of chutneys.

Best gratin toppings:

Flaked almonds

Crispy pancetta

Breadcrumbs

Pumpkin seeds

Walnuts

Gruyère cheese

A good pile of ready-salted crisps

Gratin tips

- Slice the ingredients – especially robust root veg – to the same thickness. A thick slice of potato will cook more slowly than a thin one, and you may be left with undercooked layers in the gratin. Likewise, cut less hardy ingredients – like cauliflower, broccoli, courgettes – to a larger size to withstand long cooking times.

- Adjust your cooking time to the depth of the dish you've used – a long, shallow dish will cook things faster than a deep one.

- If the top hasn't turned golden, flash it under a hot grill for 3 minutes to crisp up. If the gratin base is cooking a lot slower than the top, cover with foil until the base is cooked through, then remove to get the top golden.

- Resting your gratin after cooking allows the base time to absorb excess liquid. Gratins often taste better the next day, so make it in advance and heat it up if you have time.

A Note on Potatoes

For a gratin that will hold its shape, opt for a waxy potato such as Maris Peer or Charlotte. If you like a fluffy, almost mushy gratin, go for Rooster or King Edward for super-absorption. Desiree and Maris Piper are a happy medium between the two. I'm not very fussed, but knowing which potato you're using will give you an idea of what your gratin will look like when it's cooked. Use the same type of potato throughout the gratin – some may cook at different times. Steer clear of old, sprouting potatoes – they can be tough and musty.

Potato gratin

Potatoes have always been great mates to dairy. Throw the two together at a moment's notice and you'll have yourself a superb dinner. Potatoes are loved by all, so it's an easy one to feed friends with. When I'm feeling greedy and extravagant, I'll nip into a good cheese shop – Neal's Yard and La Fromagerie are both dangerously near work and home – just to choose the right topper for a gratin. The cheese needs to be salty and a good melter, which is why Gruyère and Parmesan do well for this. Go on … spend a while tasting before you buy, and experiment …

unsalted butter for greasing
1kg large fluffy or waxy potatoes, peeled and thinly sliced
5 sprigs of fresh thyme
300ml double cream
½ teaspoon freshly grated nutmeg
a pinch of dried chilli flakes
3 cloves of garlic, crushed
50g Parmesan cheese, grated
50g Gruyère cheese, grated

SERVES

4–6

TIME TO PREPARE

20 MINUTES

TIME TO COOK

1 HOUR 15 MINS

1. Preheat the oven to 200°C/fan 180°C/gas 6. Butter a 2 litre ovenproof dish and place a layer of the sliced potatoes in the bottom. Repeat with the rest of the potatoes, seasoning every other layer with salt, pepper and thyme.

2. Mix the cream with the nutmeg, chilli flakes and crushed garlic and season well. Whisk to evenly distribute the ingredients and pour over the potatoes. Top with the Parmesan and Gruyère, and slide into the oven to bubble and brown to golden for 1 hour 15 minutes. When the cream has thickened and has absorbed into the potatoes, and the top layer is crisp, remove from the oven. Rest for 15 minutes in a warm oven, or covered with foil, before serving.

No-cream potato gratin (Boulangère potatoes)

NO FRILLS

When cooking au gratin, it's not always necessary to pile on so much cream. Sometimes, all that is needed is the potatoes, softened onions and a well-flavoured stock. So long as the stock sits just underneath the top layer of potatoes, you'll get a deliciously crispy top, and a rich and soupy underneath.

butter or olive oil, for greasing
1kg large waxy potatoes, peeled and very thinly sliced
leaves from 5 sprigs of fresh rosemary
2 large onions, thinly sliced
½ teaspoon freshly grated nutmeg
3 cloves of garlic, crushed
1 litre chicken or vegetable stock, just boiled
50g breadcrumbs
100g Parmesan cheese, grated (optional)

1. Preheat the oven to 200°C/fan 180°C/gas 6. Grease a 2 litre ovenproof dish and place a layer of the sliced potatoes in the bottom. Season and scatter with a little of the rosemary, a quarter of the onions and a sprinkling of nutmeg. Repeat this process until you have reached the top of the dish.

2. Mix the garlic into the stock and pour it over the potatoes. Season the final layer and top with the breadcrumbs and Parmesan (if using).

3. Place in the oven, covered with foil, and bake for 1 hour 15 minutes. Leave to rest for 15 minutes in a warm oven or covered with foil, then serve.

SERVES	TIME TO PREPARE	TIME TO COOK
4–6	20 MINUTES	1 HOUR 15 MINS

Shallot, anchovy and pancetta gratin

You don't need too much going on to make a really good gratin, and they don't all need to be enormous. A few bold flavours that go well together is all that is required. If in doubt, use the rule of three:

- No cream potato, spinach, chilli
- Creamy potato, dill, fennel
- Sprouts, bacon, chestnuts
- Sweet potato, almonds, goat's cheese
- Cauliflower and broccoli cheese
- Celeriac, white cabbage, rosemary

unsalted butter, for greasing

12 banana shallots, peeled and sliced in half lengthways (blanch the shallots in just-boiled water for 2 minutes to make them easier to peel)

10 anchovies (canned in oil)

a small bunch of fresh parsley leaves, chopped

1 clove of garlic, finely chopped

100ml double cream

8 streaks of thinly sliced pancetta

1. Preheat the oven to 200°C/fan 180°C/gas 6. Butter a 1 litre ovenproof dish and lay the shallots, side by side, cut side down on the bottom of the dish. Scatter with a few anchovies and a sprinkling of the parsley leaves. Season well with salt and pepper. Lay on another layer exactly the same, then a final layer of shallots.

2. Mix the garlic into the cream and pour over the shallots. Lay the sliced pancetta over the top and place in the oven to cook for 1 hour. Once the bacon is crisp, cover the dish with a sheet of foil to carry on cooking.

3. When the shallots are cooked through, remove the dish from the oven and leave to rest for 15 minutes before serving.

SERVES	TIME TO PREPARE	TIME TO COOK
2	10 MINUTES	1 HOUR

Beetroot and sweet potato gratin

NO FRILLS

Both roots cook happily in cream and, as they soften, take on a deliciously nutty flavour. The real focus of this gratin, though, is its colour. Cut through the layers to find bright purples, hot pinks and dusky oranges. Layer it in a lovely dish – blues are a good match – and you'll have a beautiful centrepiece to the dinner table. Serve alongside a plate of excellent sausages.

unsalted butter, for greasing
4 beetroots, peeled
1–2 sweet potatoes, peeled
1 large clove of garlic
300ml double cream
2 sprigs of fresh thyme
½ teaspoon freshly grated nutmeg

SERVES	TIME TO PREPARE	TIME TO COOK
4–6	20 MINUTES	1 HOUR 15 MINS

1. Preheat the oven to 200°C/fan 180°C/gas 6. Butter a 2 litre ovenproof dish. Using a food processor, or a sharp knife, finely slice the beetroots and sweet potatoes into thin rounds.

2. Begin layering the root vegetables alternately in the dish. Start with a layer of beetroot, then sweet potato, and continue until you have used them all up.

3. Mix the garlic with the cream. Add the thyme and nutmeg and season generously.

4. Slide the dish into the oven and bake for 1 hour 15 minutes, until the top is golden, the cream has thickened and the vegetables are tender – check this by piercing them with a knife. If the knife goes through easily and the beetroot and sweet potato start to mash, it's ready. Remove and leave to cool slightly before serving. An amazing combination.

4 more ways with sweet potato

HARISSA-SPICED WEDGES
Slice an unpeeled sweet potato into wedges and rub with harissa, salt and olive oil. Roast for 35 minutes at 200°C/fan 180°C/gas 6, until golden and crisp. Serve with a yoghurt dip.

SAUSAGE AND SWEET POTATO STEW
Fry chopped sausage and chorizo in the bottom of a casserole until golden. Fry onions, garlic, and chilli and add the sweet potato. Pour over stock and chopped tomatoes and simmer gently for an hour, until the sweet potato is tender and the sauce is rich.

SWEET POTATO CURRY
Fry grated fresh root ginger, cardamom seeds, chopped chilli, grated garlic and finely chopped lemongrass in coconut oil for 2 minutes. Add sweet potato and fry, then add coconut milk and a little red curry paste. Simmer for 20 minutes, then add green beans.

SWEET POTATO DAHL
Simmer sweet potatoes and lentils in stock with cinnamon, cumin, cardamom, coriander, garlic and ginger, until the lentils are tender and the stock is absorbed. Serve with yoghurt.

Mac 'n' cheese

Macaroni cheese may be cheating a little – it's not technically a gratin, more a pasta bake, but it has all the elements to building one. Through the simple process of thickening milk into a roux and stirring through fiercely mature cheese, the dish becomes unquenchable, ravenous-making and a true favourite. Rightfully, it sits as one of the most adored plates of food in my family. And probably others.

For moments of weakness, restoration and sheer greed.

400ml whole milk
½ an onion, halved
1 clove
a pinch of freshly grated nutmeg
200g macaroni (any tubed pasta works well)
a little oil
1 tablespoon unsalted butter
25g plain flour
1 tablespoon Dijon mustard
100–150g strong Cheddar cheese, amount
    depending on how strong you like it (such
    as Westcombe mature Cheddar or Lincolnshire
    Poacher), grated or crumbled into small bits
50g breadcrumbs

SERVES

2

TIME TO PREPARE

15 MINUTES

TIME TO COOK

45 MINUTES

1. Pour the milk into a saucepan and add the onion, clove and nutmeg. Gently bring to the boil, then leave to infuse for 10 minutes.

2. Meanwhile, bring a large pan of salted water to the boil and add the macaroni. Simmer for 8 minutes, or according to the packet instructions, until *al dente*. Drain, toss with a little oil to stop it sticking, then pour into a 2 litre ovenproof dish.

3. Preheat the oven to 180°C/fan 160°C/gas 4. To make a roux for the cheese sauce, melt the butter in a large saucepan and add the flour. Fry over a low heat for 2 minutes, stirring, until the butter and flour start to make a paste, then stir in the mustard. Strain the milk into a jug, discarding the onion and cloves, and pour a little at a time into the roux, stirring in more as the sauce thickens. Whisk throughout cooking to incorporate any lumps that appear back into the sauce. When all the milk has been used, remove the pan from the heat and beat in almost all the grated cheese until smooth and creamy. Add a little salt and pepper to taste.

4. Stir the sauce through the pasta. Sprinkle the top with the remaining cheese and the breadcrumbs, then slide into the oven for 25–30 minutes, until golden and bubbling. Leave to cool slightly before serving.

Squash, blue cheese and walnut gratin

The shape, colour, sweetness and variety of squash remind me why vegetables are so very brilliant to cook with. The curvy, bell-bottomed ones, the spaceship-shaped ones, the round, the long, the spaghetti-fleshed ones are all squashes that can hold their own at the dinner table. Look for butternut squash with firm and evenly tanned skins. Scoop out the fibrous middle with a spoon and save the seeds for toasting. Serve this gratin with a roast leg of lamb in deepest autumn, or on its own, nothing else needed.

unsalted butter or oil, for greasing
1kg butternut squash (or other squash), peeled, quartered and thinly sliced
100g blue cheese (St Agur or Isle of Wight Blue)
leaves from 4 sprigs of fresh thyme
50g walnuts, crushed
3 cloves of garlic, crushed
300ml double cream

1. Preheat the oven to 200°C/fan 180°C/gas 6. Butter or oil a 2 litre ovenproof dish and place a layer of the sliced squash in the bottom. Scatter over a few crumblings of blue cheese, thyme leaves and walnuts. Repeat this process until you have reached the top of the dish.

2. Mix the garlic into the cream, season well and pour it over the squash. Top with a final sprinkling of blue cheese and the remaining crushed walnuts.

3. Place in the oven to bake for 1 hour 15 minutes, until golden and bubbling. Leave to cool slightly before serving.

SERVES

6–8

TIME TO PREPARE

20 MINUTES

TIME TO COOK

1 HOUR 15 MINS

Salt beef, celeriac, apple and potato hash

LEFTOVER LOVE

Leftover potato gratin is hard to come by, but when it's there it's fantastic cold. I love it mashed up, mixed with crispy bacon and a beaten egg, breaded and deep fried. Or sliced into deep squares, then fried in plenty of butter. Or really smutty, like this, with salt beef.

1 tablespoon olive oil
1 onion, finely diced
1 clove of garlic, crushed
300g cooked salt beef (available from delis and
    Waitrose) or corned beef, if you like it,
    pulled apart into 4cm pieces
½ a celeriac, peeled and grated
1 apple, peeled, cored and cut into small cubes
1 teaspoon English mustard
a splash of cider
leftover potato gratin (whatever you have left)

1. Heat the oil in a wide frying pan over a medium heat and add the onion. Fry for 5 minutes, then add the garlic and fry for a further 1 minute. Add the salt beef and fry until crisp. Stir in the celeriac, apple and mustard and season to taste. Splash in a drop of cider and simmer for 2 minutes, until the alcohol has evaporated.

2. Add the potato and whack up the heat until everything starts to crisp. Serve with a poached egg or pickles.

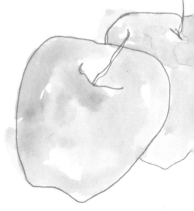

SERVES

2

TIME TO PREPARE

10 MINUTES

TIME TO COOK

10 MINUTES

'Nduja, courgette and mozzarella gratin

Move over chorizo. 'Nduja – a most scrumptious, spreadable, spicy Calabrian sausage – has wiggled its way into my kitchen and made itself a permanent fixture. Whenever I see it – on the market, online, in an Italian deli or, on the very rare occasion, in a supermarket – I grab to buy. Snap.

    'Nduja is hot, smoky and rich. You only need a little to go a long way, which is why I love it for this gratin. It moves around the whole dish, tickling the dainty new potatoes and grated courgettes, and making them bold. On first making this, I ate enough for 4 people.

1 tablespoon unsalted butter

1 red onion, sliced

2 cloves of garlic, finely chopped

2 courgettes, grated

grated zest of ½ a lemon

16 new potatoes, thinly sliced

50g 'nduja (available from Natoora, Waitrose, Unearthed and good Italian delis), torn into chunks

125g mozzarella, drained and torn

1 sprig of fresh rosemary, leaves only, chopped

200ml chicken stock

SERVES	TIME TO PREPARE	TIME TO COOK
4–6	25 MINUTES	1 HOUR

1. Preheat the oven to 200°C/fan 180°C/gas 6. Melt the butter in a large, deep ovenproof frying pan or casserole dish over a medium heat. Add the onion and fry for 10 minutes until soft. Stir in the garlic, courgettes and lemon zest and fry for another 2 minutes. Season generously with salt and pepper. Remove two-thirds of the courgette mixture from the pan and spread what's left in the pan evenly over the base.

2. Place a layer of potatoes on top of the courgettes and top with a third of the torn 'nduja, mozzarella and chopped rosemary. Repeat with another layer of courgettes, potatoes, mozzarella and 'nduja, and continue this process to the top of the dish, lightly seasoning each layer.

3. Pour the stock over the potatoes. Slide the dish into the oven and cook for 1 hour, until the top is golden and bubbling and the potatoes are tender.

Melanzane parmigiana

Aubergines are a wonderful, unusual fruit. Their thick, rubbery skin turns crisp and crunchy when grilled, and their insides, if cooked for a good amount of time, soften and sweeten. It's essential to cook the aubergines down until their middles are soft and almost translucent, otherwise they'll taste like sucking on a dry and tasteless sponge.

When it comes to tomatoes, only use them fresh if they are very ripe and sweet – out-of-season tomatoes (much of the year, sadly) rarely taste of much, so tinned plum tomatoes make a far better option. If you can find fresh ones that are juicy and red, peel them first: score a cross in the bottom of each tomato and put them into a bowl of just-boiled water for 2–4 minutes (the riper they are the more easily they will peel).

2 aubergines (500g each), sliced (go for
    a mixture of round and long)
1 tablespoon olive oil, plus extra for frying
    the aubergines
1 red onion, finely chopped
2 cloves of garlic, finely chopped
500g juicy, fresh tomatoes, peeled, or a 400g tin
    of plum tomatoes
2 sprigs of fresh oregano
a large handful of fresh basil leaves, torn
100g Parmesan cheese, grated
100g breadcrumbs (optional)

SERVES	TIME TO PREPARE	TIME TO COOK
4–6	20 MINUTES	1 HOUR

1. Rub the aubergine slices with olive oil and season. Heat a large frying pan or griddle over a medium-high heat, then lay on the aubergine and fry for 3 minutes on each side until golden and beginning to char – you may need to fry them in batches. Once you've done the lot, set them aside. They are great cooked on the barbecue too.

2. Heat the olive oil in a saucepan and add the onion. Season and gently fry over a medium heat, covered, for 10–15 minutes until soft, then add the garlic and the whole tomatoes and cook for 20 minutes, breaking up the tomatoes with a wooden spoon, until the sauce has reduced by half. Add the oregano and basil and season well.

3. Preheat the oven to 180°C/fan 160°C/gas 4. Ladle a layer of the tomato sauce into the bottom of a 2 litre ovenproof dish. Follow with a layer of aubergine and a layer of grated Parmesan. Continue this process until you've used up the remaining sauce and aubergines, finishing with a generous layer of Parmesan. Evenly scatter over the breadcrumbs (if using). Place the dish in the oven and bake for 25 minutes, until the top is golden and bubbling.

Sausage, cavolo nero and fennel lasagne

GET CREATIVE

The three ingredients I couldn't live without have made their way into this lasagne. Cavolo nero (black cabbage), with its dark, crinkly pocks and giant ear-like leaves, has great texture and chew when lightly blanched, which is well balanced with finely minced, well-seasoned pork. Sausages are well seasoned, crumbly and a great partner to cabbage. And fennel seeds give sweetness and freshness to the dish. The three are perfect for each other. You don't have to use lasagne sheets – it's a great dish without, or perhaps topped with sliced potatoes – but they add texture and division, and hold the ingredients together. And they are pasta, which is always heaven.

50g unsalted butter, plus extra for greasing

1 large cavolo nero, shredded, thick stems removed

750ml whole milk

1 banana shallot, peeled and halved

2 cloves

2 bay leaves

8 free-range pork sausages, skinned (or 500g sausage meat)

1 clove of garlic, crushed (you may not need this if your sausages are already quite garlicky – fry a little of the sausage meat first to check how it is seasoned)

1 teaspoon dried chilli flakes

1 teaspoon fennel seeds

2 tablespoons plain flour

a pinch of finely grated nutmeg

12–16 lasagne sheets

50g Parmesan cheese, grated

SERVES	TIME TO PREPARE	TIME TO COOK
4–6	20 MINUTES	1 HOUR

1. Preheat the oven to 200°C/fan 180°C/gas 6. Lightly grease a 2 litre ovenproof dish. Bring a large pan of lightly salted water to the boil and blanch the shredded cavolo nero for 2 minutes until tender and bright green. Drain and refresh under cold water. Squeeze to drain off excess water, then set aside. Pour the milk into a large saucepan and add the shallot, cloves and bay leaves. Bring to the boil, then set aside to infuse for 10 minutes.

2. Meanwhile, fry the meat from the sausages, discarding the skins, in a frying pan over a medium heat for 10 minutes, until browned and starting to caramelise. Add the garlic, chilli and fennel and cook for another minute. Set aside.

3. Melt the butter in a saucepan over a medium-low heat and add the flour. Fry for 2 minutes, stirring. Strain the warm milk and pour it, a little at a time, into the flour and butter roux, adding more as it thickens, until thick and smooth, stirring all the time. Season with nutmeg and black pepper to taste and remove from the heat.

4. Lay one fifth of the white sauce in the bottom of the ovenproof dish and top with a quarter of the pork and a quarter of the cavolo nero. Top with 3 or 4 lasagne sheets, or as many as you need to fit the dish. Layer the sheets with another fifth of white sauce, then another layer of pork and cavolo nero. Repeat this process, ending with lasagne sheets. Smooth the remaining white sauce over the top and sprinkle with the Parmesan. Slide into the oven for 30–40 minutes, until golden and bubbling and the pasta sheets are cooked.

Celery with cumin

While most consider a stick of celery to be stringy, unexciting rabbit food, I beg to differ. Celery is a must-have-in-the-fridge ingredient. Aside from stirring Bloody Marys and building a soffritto, baked celery is the business and it is incredibly easy and cheap to make. Spoon it generously alongside roast pork. Next time, swap the wine for pastis for an aniseed kick and replace the breadcrumbs with crunchy walnuts.

50g unsalted butter

1 fresh bunch of celery (about 5 sticks), trimmed of its leaves (reserve these for stocks), washed and each stick cut into 5cm lengths

1 onion, thinly sliced

2 bay leaves

100g breadcrumbs

2 tablespoons cumin seeds

75ml white wine

250ml vegetable or chicken stock

100ml double cream

25g Parmesan cheese, grated

SERVES

4 AS A SIDE

READY IN

35 MINUTES

1. Melt half the butter in a large frying pan over a medium heat, then add the celery, onion and bay leaves. Season well and gently simmer, covered, for 30 minutes, stirring occasionally, until the celery is tender.

2. Meanwhile, melt the remaining butter in a small frying pan, add the breadcrumbs and cumin and toast for 2 minutes until golden. Remove from the heat.

3. Heat the grill to medium. Pour the wine into the celery pan, bring to the boil, and simmer for 2 minutes, until the alcohol has evaporated. Add the stock, then simmer for 7 minutes to reduce by two-thirds.

4. Pour in the cream, and simmer until the sauce is thickened and syrupy. Season again to taste, then pour into a 1 litre ovenproof dish. Scatter with the spiced breadcrumbs and the grated Parmesan. Grill for 5 minutes, until bubbling, then remove and allow to cool a little before serving.

Crab gratin

Crab is a superb focus for a gratin. Thin strings of white crabmeat folded into the nutty, tart brown meat mix effortlessly into a mustard roux and sizzle under a hot grill. It's rich, yes, but that's exactly what you're looking for. The brown shrimp, while tasting sweet and delicious, offer texture. I cook it for a laid back, but treaty Sunday lunch, with a crunchy salad loaded with fresh parsley and dill to atone for the cream.

50g unsalted butter, plus extra for greasing
2 small onions, very finely chopped
1 clove of garlic, crushed
a splosh of dry sherry
2 teaspoons plain flour
200ml whole milk
1 teaspoon English mustard
a pinch of cayenne pepper
½ teaspoon Worcestershire sauce
150g soft brown crabmeat
200g white crabmeat
100g brown shrimp (optional)
a squeeze of lemon juice, or to taste

FOR THE TOPPING
100g breadcrumbs, from a coarse, stale loaf
a handful of fresh parsley leaves, chopped
40g mature Cheddar cheese, grated
a drizzle of olive oil

SERVES	TIME TO PREPARE	TIME TO COOK
4	10 MINUTES	35 MINUTES

1. Preheat the oven to 190°C/fan 170°C/gas 5. Melt the butter in a large, heavy-based saucepan over a medium-low heat. Add the onion and garlic and sweat for 10 minutes, covered, until softened. Pour in the sherry and simmer for 2 minutes to evaporate the alcohol. Stir in the flour and coat the onions. Fry for 2 minutes, then gradually pour in the milk as the sauce thickens, stirring all the while. Stir in the mustard, cayenne pepper and Worcestershire sauce, adding more to taste, if you like. Bring to a gentle simmer then remove from the heat.

2. Fold the brown and white crabmeat and the shrimp (if using) into the sauce. Season well with salt, pepper and lemon juice to taste, then pour into a 1 litre ovenproof dish. Mix the breadcrumbs with the parsley and cheese and sprinkle over the crab. Drizzle with olive oil, then slide on to a baking tray and bake in the oven for 20 minutes, or until golden and bubbling. Serve immediately.

Potato, lemon and herb tortilla

LEFTOVER LOVE

For an authentic Spanish tortilla, thinly sliced raw potatoes are crisped in a pan with sizzling olive oil. They are tossed, still hot, in beaten egg and poured back into the pan to set over a low heat. It's one of the most wonderful things.

Here, the potatoes are already cooked so they just need a quick fly around the heat. Herbs in vast quantities wilt down to almost nothing but leave a liveliness, perked up even more by a squeeze of lemon juice. Be prepared to get messy first time round but don't panic if the juices run when you flip the tortilla, just pour them back into the pan. A joy to eat, morning, noon or night.

6 large free-range eggs

a small handful of fresh mint, parsley or tarragon, finely chopped

4 tablespoons extra virgin olive oil, plus extra to serve

1 onion, finely sliced

100g leftover potato gratin (or 4 small waxy potatoes, cooked)

a squeeze of lemon juice, to serve

SERVES	TIME TO PREPARE	TIME TO COOK
4 AS TAPAS	**10** MINUTES	**35** MINUTES

1. Lightly beat the eggs in a large mixing bowl, season well with salt and pepper, stir in the chopped mint, parsley or tarragon and put to one side.

2. Heat 1 tablespoon of the olive oil in a deep, 20cm non-stick frying pan over a medium heat. Fry the onion for 10–15 minutes, until softened and golden, and set aside. Pour in the rest of the olive oil to heat up, then, when hot, add the potato and fry for another 5–10 minutes, until beginning to crisp.

3. Mix the potatoes and onions into the beaten egg, then pour into the hot frying pan. Fry for 5 minutes over a medium-high heat, stirring at the beginning, until the omelette is cooked halfway up the pan and still wobbly on top. Place a plate on top of the pan and flip the pan over so that the cooked part of the omelette faces down. It'll be sloppy but that's all part of the fun! Slide the omelette back into the pan and fry for another 5 minutes. Transfer to a board or plate, drizzle with a little olive oil and a squeeze of lemon juice, sprinkle with flaked sea salt and slice to serve.

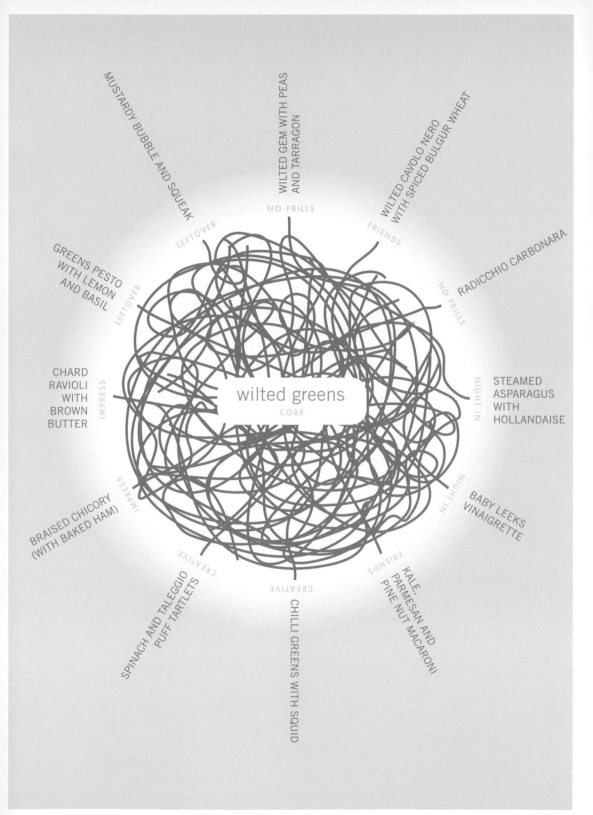

MUSTARDY BUBBLE AND SQUEAK

WILTED GEM WITH PEAS AND TARRAGON

WILTED CAVOLO NERO WITH SPICED BULGUR WHEAT

NO FRILLS

FRIENDS

GREENS PESTO WITH LEMON AND BASIL

LEFTOVER

LEFTOVER

RADICCHIO CARBONARA

NO FRILLS

CHARD RAVIOLI WITH BROWN BUTTER

IMPRESS

wilted greens
CORE

NIGHT IN

STEAMED ASPARAGUS WITH HOLLANDAISE

IMPRESS

NIGHT IN

BRAISED CHICORY (WITH BAKED HAM)

BABY LEEKS VINAIGRETTE

CREATIVE

FRIENDS

SPINACH AND TALEGGIO PUFF TARTLETS

CREATIVE

KALE, PARMESAN AND PINE NUT MACARONI

CHILLI GREENS WITH SQUID

Wilted Greens

You'll quickly see throughout this chapter that by 'greens' I do not mean the colour. Greens, in this case, can be red, white and deep purple as well as deep and muted shades of lime, grass and jade.

Here, the 'greens' wheel hails the all-creative leafy vegetable. It spins around the mustardy brassicas: cabbages, kales and spring greens, pointy, curly, of many layers. It explores bitter, crunchy chicory and radicchio, oniony leeks, nutty asparagus, and sweet salads, like lettuce, spinach and chard. These leaves are mostly water, so when gently cooked they wilt down to expose vibrant colours and earthy flavours.

When buying or harvesting greens, look for firm, tight leaves and avoid those that are slimy. To wilt, you can gently fry, blanch or steam – it's up to you. You can eat them on their own, stir them into sauces, or stuff them into pasta. The greens in each recipe are interchangeable. I have left some out which need a mention, though some appear in other recipe wheels.

Look for

Wild garlic
Cauliflower leaves
Sprouts
Beetroot leaves
Kohlrabi
Broccoli

Greens tips

• Greens need thorough washing before you wilt them – some are full of grit, especially leeks – so rinse well and pat dry before use.

• Greens can be cooked in advance, halfway to wilted, then reheated to serve. Freeze cooked greens in batches and heat from frozen.

• Don't be tempted to overcook – this is a celebration of greens, not a nostalgia for sludgy school dinners.

Wilted greens three ways

CORE

These three ways of cooking apply to any of the greens group. Remove thick stalks from cabbages and chard, trim an outer layer and the root from leeks, and snap the woody ends from asparagus – boil these separately or save them for stocks and risottos. Spinach and lettuce need less time, as they have a very high water content – sometimes the best way of wilting these is to pour hot water over them through a colander. Wilt larger leaves until soft with a slight bite.

FRY

3 tablespoons olive oil
1 clove of garlic, finely chopped
approx. 1kg greens, roughly chopped (washed thoroughly, then dried off in tea towels or in a salad spinner)

Heat the olive oil in a large pan over a medium-low heat and add the garlic. Cook for 2 minutes, then add the greens, a batch at a time, and stir for 5 minutes, until tender. Take off the heat and remove the greens with tongs to serve. Reserve any juices for salad dressings.

BLANCH

approx. 1kg greens (not delicate, watery leaves), roughly chopped (washed thoroughly, then dried off in tea towels or in a salad spinner)

Bring a large pan of salted water or stock to the boil. Add the greens, then turn down the heat and simmer for 5 minutes, until bright and tender. Drain and refresh under cold water.

STEAM

approx. 1kg greens, roughly chopped (washed thoroughly, then dried off in tea towels or in a salad spinner)

Bring a large pan quarter full with water to the boil. Turn down heat, rest a steamer or colander on the pan (not touching the water), add greens, cover and steam for 5 minutes, until tender.

SERVES

4

READY IN

15 MINUTES

Wilted Gem lettuce with peas and tarragon

This is a favourite side to Sunday night roast chicken. You want to quickly blanch the leaves in the stock so that they just wilt but still have crunch. Keep the Gem hearts whole if you like and stir through a dollop of crème fraîche to enrich. For extra bite, fry pancetta to crisp before adding the shallot.

1 tablespoon olive oil
1 shallot, finely sliced
2 cloves of garlic, sliced
50ml chicken or vegetable stock
300g petits pois, fresh or frozen
4 Little Gem lettuces, pulled into separate leaves
leaves from a few sprigs of fresh tarragon, chopped

1. Heat the oil in a large pan over a medium-low heat. Add the shallot and fry gently for 5 minutes, until just soft. Add the garlic, fry for another minute, then pour in the chicken stock and bring to a simmer. Add the peas and cook for 2 minutes, until tender.

2. Turn off the heat, add the lettuce leaves, season well with salt and pepper and toss with tongs to just wilt the salad in the hot stock. Pour the peas and lettuce into a shallow serving bowl and stir in the chopped tarragon before serving.

SERVES

4 AS A SIDE

READY IN

20 MINUTES

Wilted cavolo nero with spiced bulgur wheat

Perfect packed lunch material. Cabbage – in this case black cabbage – shrinks a little when cooked, but wilted it can be stretched with other ingredients to feed people for days. I've gone off couscous somewhat, so bulgur takes its place. Quinoa, barley couscous and buckwheat are other good alternatives.

1.5kg cavolo nero leaves, thick stems removed
1 tablespoon extra virgin olive oil,
    plus extra to serve
3 onions, finely sliced
1 cinnamon stick
a strand of blade mace or a few gratings of nutmeg
1 tablespoon honey
2 tablespoons cumin seeds
1 clove of garlic, crushed
500g bulgur wheat
chicken or vegetable stock, to cover
natural yoghurt, for dolloping

1. Bring a pan of salted water to the boil and add the cavolo nero. Simmer for 3 minutes, then drain and refresh under cold water. Set aside to cool.

2. Heat the oil in the pan over a medium heat and add the onion with the cinnamon stick, blade mace or nutmeg, and honey. Fry, uncovered, for 15 minutes, until completely soft and caramelised. Season well, then stir in the cumin seeds and garlic.

3. Add the bulgur wheat and pour over enough stock to cover. Bring to a simmer and cook for 10 minutes, covered, until tender and the liquid has been absorbed. Leave to rest for a few minutes, then fluff up with a fork. Toss through the wilted cavolo nero and season to taste. Arrange on a large platter and drizzle generously with olive oil. Serve with flatbreads and a dollop of yoghurt.

SERVES

6

READY IN

40 MINUTES

Radicchio carbonara

NO FRILLS

Radicchio has spirit. Its strong bitter tang strikes gold to those who love a glass of Campari, like chicory in salads and enjoy black tea without milk. Tangy radicchio deserves to be paired with things that are syrupy, salty and sweet to really show it off. Here it is wilted down with cured pancetta, garlic and plenty of Parmesan, and caramelised with a cheeky knob of butter. Tomorrow, it'll be fried down and tossed with balsamic vinegar and peppery, sweet basil and eaten with a ripe tomato salad.

400g spaghetti or linguine

a little olive oil

a 250g piece of best dry-cure pancetta, roughly chopped, fat on, or 8 thin slices

2 large heads of radicchio, thinly shredded

1 clove of garlic, crushed

a knob of butter

a good splash of white wine

4 large free-range egg yolks

50g Parmesan cheese, plus extra to serve

chopped fresh parsley leaves, to serve

SERVES

4

READY IN

30 MINUTES

1. Bring a deep saucepan of salted water to the boil. Add the spaghetti or linguine and simmer for 8 minutes, or according to the packet instructions, until *al dente*. Drain, reserving 1 tablespoon of the pasta water, and refresh under cold water to stop it cooking. Drizzle with a little olive oil, and set aside while you make the sauce.

2. Fry the pancetta in a frying pan over a medium-high heat with a drop of olive oil until crisp. Remove the pancetta from the pan, then add the radicchio to the pan with the garlic and butter and fry for 2 minutes. Pour in the wine and simmer for 4 minutes, until the alcohol has burnt off and the radicchio has wilted and is beginning to caramelise.

3. Whisk the egg yolks and Parmesan together in a bowl or jug. Season generously with salt and pepper.

4. Toss the pasta through the pancetta and radicchio with the reserved pasta water. Remove from the heat, then pour in the egg mixture and quickly and evenly toss through. Serve immediately, with a little extra grated Parmesan and chopped parsley.

Steamed asparagus with hollandaise

There is little more satisfying than snapping the first asparagus spear of the spring season. Its arrival in mid April – if all goes well – is true excitement. Almost every night, I carry home armfuls of bunches to drizzle in butter, bake with anchovies or dunk in buttery hollandaise. The rule is to gobble as much as you can until it peels off in June.

A note or two about hollandaise. Make sure the temperature of the bowl over the water doesn't get too hot or the eggs will curdle. Work on a very low heat and whisk in the butter, little by little, making sure all the sauce keeps moving around the bowl.

Saving a curdled hollandaise is not easy, but try removing it from the heat and beating it gradually into another egg yolk.

Once emulsified, hollandaise doesn't heat up very well, but it can be kept warm in a thermos or in a bowl, covered with clingfilm, placed over a pan of warm water.

3 tablespoons white wine vinegar
2 white peppercorns, crushed
1 bay leaf
2 large free-range egg yolks
110g unsalted butter, chilled and diced
a good squeeze of lemon juice, or to taste
16 fresh and crunchy asparagus spears,
    snapped off ends

SERVES

2

READY IN

20 MINUTES

1. Heat the white wine vinegar in a saucepan over a gentle heat with the peppercorns and bay leaf and reduce to 1 tablespoon's worth. Strain the vinegar into a heatproof bowl and whisk in the egg yolks with one cube of butter. Set the bowl over a pan of barely simmering water, making sure the bowl doesn't touch the water. Keep whisking, adding one cube of butter at a time, until the sauce is thick and creamy. (Remove from the heat and continue to whisk if the water gets too hot.) Squeeze in the lemon juice and keep warm until ready to serve (see opposite).

2. When ready to serve, bring a pan of lightly salted water to the boil and balance a steamer or colander on top. Add the asparagus and steam for 5 minutes, until tender. Serve immediately, or refresh under cold water, dry with a tea towel and set aside. Serve on a plate and pour over plenty of the warm hollandaise.

Baby leeks vinaigrette

Poor man's asparagus, as it's often called, doused in this sharp and salty dressing, is the perfect night-in starter. Gently blanching leeks gives a completely different effect to frying. It brings out the sweetness in the leek, and peeling back its translucent layers reveals a tender middle. I like a slight squeaky chew – the older the crop, the more fibrous they can be – but baby leeks can be softer and easier to manage, though you'll still need a sharp knife to cut through the layers.

If you prefer a simpler vinaigrette without the eggs, whisk together the mustard, vinegar and olive oil and mix with the capers. Anchovies and cornichons are extras for those who crave more salt and vinegar.

6 baby leeks or 2 large leeks (about 150g)
1 large free-range egg and 1 large free-range egg yolk
1 teaspoon Dijon mustard
1 teaspoon white wine vinegar
50ml light-flavoured olive oil or half sunflower, half extra virgin olive oil
2 tablespoons capers, drained, rinsed, patted dry and finely chopped
1 tablespoon chopped cornichons (optional)
1 anchovy, finely chopped (optional)
2 sprigs of fresh tarragon, leaves picked
hazelnuts, toasted and chopped, to serve

SERVES

2 AS A STARTER

READY IN

30 MINUTES

1. Trim the leeks, removing any tough outer layers and slicing off the green tips and root. Halve lengthways, and again widthways if large. Wash thoroughly to rinse out any grit.

2. Bring a pan of lightly salted water to the boil and add the leeks. Simmer for 8–10 minutes, until the leeks are tender when pierced with a knife. Remove the leeks with a slotted spoon, blot with kitchen paper and leave to cool at room temperature.

3. Bring the same pan of water to the boil again and lower in the whole egg. Boil for 6 minutes until soft-boiled. Remove from the pan and rinse under cold water to cool, then peel. Set aside.

4. Put the egg yolk into a large bowl and whisk in the mustard and vinegar. Season well with salt and pepper. Slowly whisk in oil until the dressing is thickened and emulsified into a thin mayonnaise. Fold in the capers, cornichons and anchovy (if using) and tarragon and roughly crush in the boiled egg with a fork.

5. Divide the leeks between 2 plates. Spoon the vinaigrette over the leeks and sprinkle with chopped hazelnuts.

Kale, Parmesan and pine nut macaroni

There's a cracking village shop on the Isle of Wight where you buy local produce, still dirty and misshapen, and giant sourdough loaves in abundance. It used to be the place you picked up sherbet dip dabs and counted pennies for foamy teeth.

On an unusually sunny weekend in February we ate a bagful of the shop's kale, wilted, then fried, and tossed into creamy macaroni, on a table out in the garden. Despite being an autumn/winter vegetable it can be surprisingly lively and uplifting. At other times of the year, use purple sprouting broccoli, artichokes or watercress.

400g kale, thick stems removed and leaves chopped
400g macaroni
2 teaspoons olive oil, plus extra for drizzling
2 cloves of garlic, crushed
3 anchovies (canned in oil), chopped (optional)
50g Parmesan cheese, plus extra to serve
150ml double cream
a small handful of fresh basil leaves, torn
grated zest of ½ a lemon
4 tablespoons pine nuts, toasted

1. Bring a large saucepan of salted water to the boil. Add the kale and simmer for 3 minutes, until it is just tender and bright green. Remove with tongs and refresh in ice-cold water, then wrap the leaves in a clean tea towel to dry.

2. Bring the water to the boil again, then add the macaroni with a splash of olive oil and cook for 8 minutes, or according to packet instructions, until *al dente*.

SERVES	TIME TO PREPARE	TIME TO COOK
4–6	10 MINUTES	20 MINUTES

3. Meanwhile, heat the olive oil in a large frying pan over a medium heat and add the garlic and anchovies (if using). Fry for 1 minute, until the anchovies start to dissolve, then add the Parmesan and cream. Let the cream simmer for a few minutes to thicken. Season generously with salt and pepper.

4. Drain the pasta and stir into the cream with the kale, basil, lemon zest and pine nuts. The pasta will absorb the cream as it sits, so don't worry if the sauce is loose to begin with. Serve on warm plates and top with extra Parmesan and olive oil.

4 more ways with kale

KALE AND WILD MUSHROOM PIE
Blanch kale, drain and squeeze. Fry wild mushrooms in butter until crisp and stir in chopped fresh tarragon. Drain the fat from the mushrooms into a clean pan, adding more butter if necessary, and make a roux with flour and milk. Stir in the kale, some mustard and the mushrooms and pour into a pie dish. Top with puff pastry and bake until crisp.

CRISPY KALE
Pour 2.5cm of vegetable oil into a pan. Heat to 160°C and drop in blanched and dried kale leaves. Fry until crisp, then remove with a slotted spoon. Use to top stir-fries and soups.

KALE AND GRUYÈRE TART
Mix eggs with cream, fresh parsley and cooked kale. Season generously and stir in grated Gruyère. Fill a blind-baked tart case and bake until set.

POACHED EGG AND KALE TOAST
Spread chilli jam on thickly sliced sourdough toasts. Top with blanched, seasoned kale and a poached egg for a speedy, scrumptious breakfast, lunch or supper.

Chilli greens with squid

GET CREATIVE

Spring greens go with anything – even just a good amount of salt and pepper will liven them up. It's all too tempting to veer these greens east and go for a more Asian vibe, but Italian style rules. In the event that you do want to go down the fish sauce/soy route, use pak choi, add rice wine vinegar, fish sauce and sugar to taste and toss with pan-fried tofu.

sunflower oil, for frying

500g squid, cleaned, then sliced
(keep the tentacles!)

100g plain flour, seasoned generously with salt and pepper

1 tablespoon extra virgin olive oil

2 cloves of garlic, sliced

2 fresh red chillies, finely chopped, or 1 teaspoon dried chilli flakes

4 large, juicy anchovies (canned in oil)

1.5kg spring greens, washed and dried, sliced

1 tablespoon red wine vinegar

lemon wedges, to serve

SERVES

4

READY IN

30 MINUTES

1. Fill a deep saucepan two-thirds full with sunflower oil and set over a medium-high heat. Heat to 180°C, checking with a digital thermometer, or until a piece of bread browns in 40 seconds. Keep it at this heat – this may mean turning the heat down, on and off, to keep the temperature stable.

2. Meanwhile, pat the squid dry with kitchen paper. Dust the squid with the flour and individually lower them into the hot oil with tongs. Hold each squid down in the oil for a few seconds before dropping it in – this will prevent it sticking to the bottom of the pan. Fry the squid in batches for 3–4 minutes, until crisp and golden. Remove with a slotted spoon and place on kitchen paper to drain off excess oil. Loosely cover with foil to keep warm.

3. Heat the olive oil in a pan over a medium-low heat and add the garlic, chilli and anchovy. Add the greens and let them wilt, moving them around the pan, for 5 minutes, until softened. Add the red wine vinegar and season well with salt and pepper. Serve alongside the squid and a few lemon wedges.

Spinach and taleggio puff tartlets

Dearest little things to pack in your
knapsack. Or to serve up for brunch.
Crunch all in one bite.

300g spinach, washed
plain flour, for dusting
1 x 320g sheet of ready-rolled all-butter puff pastry
1 tablespoon Dijon mustard
4 medium free-range eggs, plus 3 egg yolks
50ml double cream
100g taleggio cheese, torn into 12 pieces
a small bunch of fresh thyme, leaves stripped

1. Preheat the oven to 200°C/fan 180°C/gas 6. Place the spinach in a colander, or keep it in the one it has been washed in. Pour over boiling water to wilt. Alternatively, fry the spinach with a little olive oil in a large saucepan over a medium heat until wilted. Leave to cool slightly, then squeeze out excess liquid.

2. Unroll the pastry on to a floured surface and cut into 12 squares large enough to fit a 12-hole cupcake tin. Line the tins with the pastry. Brush the mustard on to the pastry.

3. Beat the whole eggs with 2 of the egg yolks, then stir in the spinach and cream. Season generously. Divide between the pastry cups, then top with the cheese and thyme. Whisk the remaining egg yolk and use to glaze the exposed pastry.

4. Cook for 15 minutes, until golden and set. Cover with foil if the tarts brown too quickly. Cool slightly, then turn out. Serve warm or cold.

MAKES	TIME TO PREPARE	TIME TO COOK
12 TARTLETS	10 MINUTES	20 MINUTES

Braised chicory

I like choosing vegetables that look interesting – rarely uniform, and full of colour. Chicory are like brushes, dipped in paint; when wilted, the colour fades, like washing the brushes clean. Combine red- and green-tipped chicory to braise and wilt. Sharp flavours in chicory, like radicchio from the same family, suits sugar, which is where the Madeira makes its mark. Likewise, go for sweet sherry, or Marsala.

100g unsalted butter
8 red and white chicory, halved
1 small head of fennel, sliced (fronds reserved)
juice of 1 lemon
2 tablespoons Madeira

1. Melt the butter in a large saucepan over a medium-low heat until brown and nutty. Add the chicory and fennel and fry gently for 10 minutes, until beginning to soften and turn a golden colour.

2. Add the lemon juice and the Madeira, and season well. Simmer gently, covered, for 30 minutes, until wilted and gooey. Top with the reserved fennel fronds and serve with baked ham (see overleaf).

SERVES	TIME TO PREPARE	TIME TO COOK
4–6	10 MINUTES	50 MINUTES

Baked ham to go with braised chicory

(because I love them together)

You can cook the soaked ham the day before, then glaze and bake it the next day to serve with the braised chicory (see page 217).

3kg smoked gammon (soaked in water overnight)
1 large onion, quartered
2 carrots, peeled and roughly chopped
2 bay leaves
2 star anise
a pinch of blade mace
10 black peppercorns
1 litre medium dry cider
1 litre ginger ale
12 cloves
5 tablespoons runny honey
2 teaspoons ground ginger
1 teaspoon English mustard powder
2–3 tablespoons demerara sugar

SERVES

8–10

TIME TO PREPARE

20 MINUTES + COOLING

TIME TO COOK

6–7 HOURS

1. Place the ham in a large saucepan and cover with fresh water. Bring to the boil, then drain off the water. Put the onion, carrots, bay leaves, star anise, mace and peppercorns into the pan with the ham. Pour in the cider and ginger ale and enough water to completely cover the ham.

2. Put on the hob over a high heat and bring to the boil. Simmer for 15 minutes. Cover, transfer to the oven and cook for 4–5 hours at 140°C/fan 120°C/gas 1 until the ham has no resistance when you stick a skewer into its centre and the fat slides easily from the meat. The cider stock will taste sweet and fantastic. DO NOT throw it away – strain and use for gravy! (Stop here, remove the ham from the stock and leave in the fridge for up to 2 days, well wrapped, before continuing the recipe.)

3. Preheat the oven to 180°C/fan 160°C/gas 4. Using a sharp knife, carefully peel the skin away from the cooked ham, leaving as much of the fat behind as you can. Score the fat in a criss-cross pattern and press the cloves into the crosses. Mix the honey with the ginger and mustard powder, then smear all over the ham. Sprinkle with the demerara sugar, then roast in the oven for 45 minutes to 1 hour until sticky and piping hot throughout.

Chard ravioli with brown butter

COOK TO IMPRESS

Filling pasta: another road for wilted greens, their versatility never ending. Chard – Swiss, ruby, wavy or rainbow – is a favourite: its verdant fronds, like spinach, are easily wilted to fold into any dish, or scrunch up into a juicy middle for fresh ravioli. Lively, glowing stems have crunch and so take longer to soften – cook them separately to avoid puncturing the pasta dough, and offer them up as a delicious side. When using greens as part of a pasta filling, you want to squeeze out as much water as possible so that the other filling ingredients don't become too loose. The filling wants to be firm enough to hold its shape within the ravioli.

I've defaulted to grating in hard pecorino and mixing it with light, crumbly ricotta to hold the chard. It oozes as you cut open the pasta, and you're left with a sauce that melts into the nutty brown butter. Herbs – without stalks – are great blended into the mix for freshness. Go for flavours that are not too overpowering – you want to have a balance in flavour for such a delicate dish and still be able to taste the pasta dough.

Making homemade pasta is a rare treat. I'm always surprised by how quick it is to make – no longer than a chicken takes to roast in the oven – and I'm never disappointed when I devour a plateful for dinner. If it doesn't strike you as a night to get rolling, the filling mixture is delicious tossed through orechiette or farfalle.

MAKES

12 RAVIOLI

TIME TO PREPARE

50 MINUTES + RESTING

TIME TO COOK

20 MINUTES

250g Tipo 'OO' flour (finely ground from hard
     wheat flour which strengthens the pasta and
     makes it silky), plus extra for dusting

2 large free-range eggs, plus 1 free-range egg yolk

¼ teaspoon whole milk

1 tablespoon olive oil

1 clove of garlic, crushed

400g chard, washed thoroughly, crunchy stems
     removed and cooked separately (or beetroot
     leaves, spinach and wild garlic)

40g pecorino, grated, plus extra to serve

4 tablespoons ricotta (Laverstoke Park make a
     good ricotta that is well drained – if you
     can find it, use it so the filling doesn't get
     too wet, otherwise take a little time to drain
     your ricotta through a fine colander or sieve
     before using)

100g unsalted butter

1. Gather up the flour into a large bowl or on the surface of a smooth wooden table, and make a well in the centre. Add the eggs and egg yolk to the well and whisk with a fork, slowly pulling in the flour from the sides until you have a loose dough, adding a little milk as you go. Push any excess flour aside – you may not need to use all of it.

2. Bring the dough together and knead – pushing the dough away, folding and pulling. Turn the dough clockwise as you knead and repeat for 8–10 minutes, until the dough feels smooth yet firm. Stick your finger into the dough; if it comes away clean, it's ready. Wrap the dough in clingfilm or place it in a freezer bag, pushing out the air from the bag, and rest it at room temperature (no warmer) for at least 15 minutes and up to 2 hours. This allows the gluten to develop and makes the dough stretchier and easier to roll.

3. Meanwhile, heat the olive oil in a large pan with the garlic over a medium-low heat. Fry for 1 minute, making sure the garlic doesn't burn, then add the chard. Fry for 5 minutes, until wilted, then cool slightly and squeeze out as much excess water as possible. Allow to cool.

4. Mix the pecorino and ricotta into the chard and season generously with salt and pepper. The mix should not be too wet – if it is, add a little flour. Set aside in the fridge until needed.

5. Remove the dough from its clingfilm and slice it in half, wrapping one half in clingfilm again. If using a pasta machine, dust your table with flour, making sure you have plenty of space on the side that the pasta comes out, then feed the dough through the widest setting. Fold the dough on itself, then push through again. Repeat this process, moving through all the settings until you reach the narrowest. You want the pasta to be thin enough to be almost translucent – you should be able to see newspaper print through it. If rolling by hand, lightly flour the surface and, using a rolling pin, roll out the dough, pushing away and pulling towards you once before turning the dough clockwise. Repeat this until the pasta is translucent. This should take no longer than 15 minutes. Cover the sheet of pasta with a damp, not wet, tea towel and roll out the wrapped dough.

6. Working as fast as you can so the pasta doesn't dry out, cut the rolled dough into 24 discs with a 6cm cookie cutter and lay on a tray lined with a damp, but not wet, tea towel or kitchen paper. Fill half the discs with 1 teaspoon of the chard filling. Place another disc on top and, brushing a tiny drop of water around the edges, press the two discs of pasta together. Sprinkle with flour and cover with another damp tea towel. Transfer to the fridge to rest for up to 3 hours until you want to serve.

7. To make the brown butter, melt the butter in a pan over a medium heat and slowly simmer until the butter turns an amber colour and starts to smell nutty. Keep warm.

8. Bring a large pan of salted water to the boil. Drop in the ravioli (you may need to do this in batches) and cook for 3–4 minutes, until *al dente*. Remove with a slotted spoon on to kitchen paper to drain excess water, then divide on to warm plates. Drizzle with the brown butter, season with fine sea salt and sprinkle with the extra grated pecorino. Serve with the cooked chard stalks (if using).

Greens pesto with lemon and basil

LEFTOVER LOVE

Leftover greens often get left in the back of the fridge to go soggy, flat and rancid. They aren't the easiest things to perk up, especially when you've just had the pleasure of eating them fresh. The best way to keep them happy is to drain any juices and seal them tightly in a freezer bag. Freezing is an excellent keeper too. Simply blanched, undressed greens taste just as good after being frozen for a month.

If, like me, you can't bear to waste, then whizzing into pesto is the solution! Lemon lifts, nuts smooth and olive oil keeps it living a little bit longer. Ready in 20 and alive again.

100g leftover cooked greens
(or fresh greens, wilted)
2 cloves of garlic, chopped
50g Parmesan or pecorino cheese
a large bunch of fresh basil leaves
grated zest and juice of 1 lemon
2 tablespoons chopped hazelnuts or
macadamia nuts
50ml olive oil

MAKES

300ML

READY IN

20 MINUTES

1. Squeeze any excess liquid from the greens and place in a food processor. Whiz, then remove and squeeze again. Place them back in the food processor with the garlic, Parmesan, basil, lemon zest and juice and the nuts and blend to a pulp.

2. Gradually pour in the olive oil while whizzing until the pesto emulsifies. Season generously and serve on top of soups or with hunks of bread. (If you don't have a food processor, finely chop the ingredients as much as possible, mix, whisk in the olive oil and season.)

Mustardy bubble and squeak

This is the best recipe for using up unwanted scraps. There are classic recipes for bubble and squeak – traditionally made with veg leftovers from a Sunday roast, bubbling and squeaking in the pan – but they aren't really to be kept to. Play around according to what you have. If you've got a bowl of mashed potatoes, or cooked potatoes to mash, all the better, just make sure they have time out of the fridge to soften before frying. You want to have a golden crust and soft middle. To follow the retro route, I like crisping up and stirring in a bit of corned beef, or flaking through smoked fish.

400g floury potatoes, unpeeled and quartered
    (go for fluffy Rooster, Maris Piper or
    King Edward if you have them)
2 tablespoons snipped fresh chives
1 teaspoon chopped fresh tarragon
1 teaspoon Dijon mustard
1 tablespoon wholegrain mustard
2 tablespoons whole milk
a handful of frozen or cooked peas (optional)
50–100g leftover greens, shredded
    (or fresh ones, wilted)
a knob or two of unsalted butter

SERVES

2 AS A MAIN

READY IN

40 MINUTES

1. Place the potatoes in a large pan of cold salted water and bring to the boil. Cook for 15–20 minutes, until tender. Drain and set back on the heat to steam off excess liquid. Remove from the heat and roughly mash the potatoes. Stir through the remaining ingredients apart from the butter and season generously.

2. Melt a knob of butter in your pan over a medium heat. When the butter is bubbling, add the potato and press into the pan with a fish slice. Ideally you want the patty to come flush with the edges of a small frying pan to make it easier to flip – a 20cm omelette pan works well. Fry for 10 minutes over a medium heat, until a crust has formed. Place a flat board or plate over the pan and, flipping, turn out the bubble and squeak. Add a little more butter to the pan if necessary and slide it back in. Fry for another 10 minutes on the other side until golden, then slice to serve.

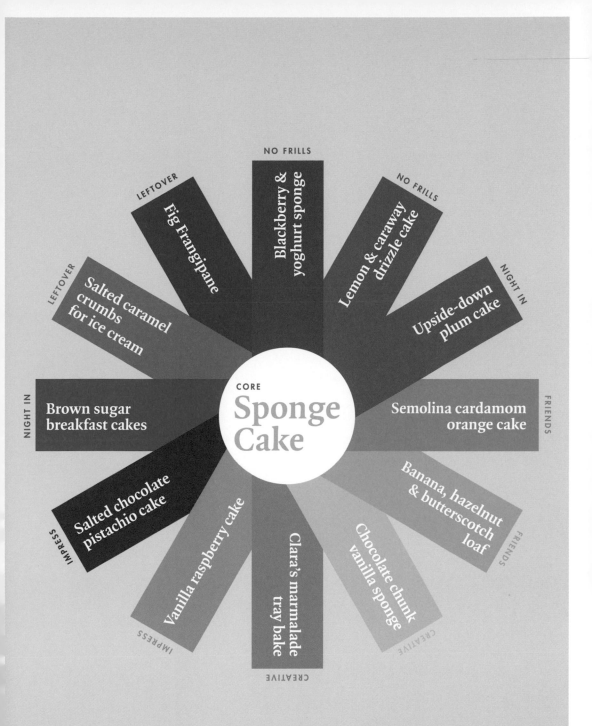

NO FRILLS

Blackberry & yoghurt sponge

LEFTOVER

Fig Frangipane

NO FRILLS

Lemon & caraway drizzle cake

LEFTOVER

Salted caramel crumbs for ice cream

NIGHT IN

Upside-down plum cake

NIGHT IN

Brown sugar breakfast cakes

CORE

Sponge Cake

Semolina cardamom orange cake

FRIENDS

IMPRESS

Salted chocolate pistachio cake

Banana, hazelnut & butterscotch loaf

FRIENDS

Vanilla raspberry cake

Clara's marmalade tray bake

Chocolate chunk vanilla sponge

IMPRESS

CREATIVE

CREATIVE

Sponge Cake

Once you know the formula, cake baking is easy. It's often said that you can't veer off with cake recipes, willy-nilly, but I invariably disagree. OK, bear the key tips in mind with each cake you make, and pay attention to why what is going where. But, there's nothing more satisfying – like in all cooking, really – than coming up with an idea and it working out well. As a general rule, measure out equal parts fat (this can be a mixture of butter, oil, yoghurts, soured creams and buttermilk) to sugar, flour and eggs. Keep this tip to hand – with a little baking powder and vanilla extract – and you can whip up lovely cakes, experimenting a little each time, without consulting a recipe.

Fruit appears heavily in this chapter – I can't resist sweet and sour together. It softens the batter and surprises with little squidges of juice. Lemon sharpens up the sponge, and balances cakes that could otherwise be too sweet.

Chocolate cannot be ignored either – naughty, gooey and rich – especially when broken into a vanilla sponge and smothered in peanut butter, or mixed with pistachios. Find ways for cheeky leftovers too. They become a magnificent ingredient in their own right and can transform a pudding. Time to play.

Tips for sweet success

- Grease your tin and line the bottom with greaseproof paper, then dust the sides with flour (or cocoa for chocolate cakes). There is nothing more infuriating than leaving half your sponge stuck to the tin!

- Always make sure all your ingredients are at room temperature – and your butter is soft. It makes the batter much easier and quicker to beat and less likely to curdle.

- Beat the sugar and butter for around 4 minutes before beating in the eggs and folding in the flour. This fluffs up and puts air through the fats in the butter and dissolves the sugar, which will help lighten and rise the batter. If the kitchen is warm, this will happen quicker. Melting butter gives a denser loaf, as does olive oil, as fewer air bubbles form than when you use hard fats – with these, there is less need to gently fold in flour.

- Stand mixers are a brilliant thing to have if you like making cakes often. They lift the batter, whisk it well and cut out most of the hard work. They are not essential, though. A hand whisk is good, and beating by hand gives you a feel for how the batter develops.

- Dust your fruit with flour, or chop it up into small pieces, to stop it sinking through the batter.

- Give the cake room to rise in the tin. Don't fill it more than two-thirds full.

- Make sure you know the correct temperature of your oven and where the hot spots are before you bake. Oven thermometers cost from £5 to £30 – it is well worth investing.

- Don't be tempted to open the oven while the cake is baking. It's lovely to watch the cake rise and colour, but the loss in temperature and sudden burst of air can cause the batter to sink.

- Leave cakes to cool completely on a wire rack before icing. Icing spread onto a cake that is still warm will melt, absorb into the sponge or just slide off.

Sponge cake with mascarpone icing

CORE

This is the perfect vehicle – light and fluffy – for carrying flavours, colourings and fruity fillings. It's delicious on its own too. If you like, spread the centre with jam and ripe raspberries and mix the icing with zesty lemon. I like to make a blueberry compote to fill the middle: heat 200g blueberries in a pan with 1 tablespoon of sugar until just soft and beginning to lose their shape. Allow the cake and blueberries to cool before icing. Buttermilk gives a slight tang to the sponge. It is high in acid and helps to moisten the cake and, though low in fat, it makes up for using less butter.

175g unsalted butter, softened, plus extra
    for greasing
250g caster sugar
1 teaspoon vanilla extract
4 medium free-range eggs, at room temperature
250g plain flour
1 teaspoon baking powder
¼ teaspoon fine sea salt
3 tablespoons buttermilk (about 50ml)

FOR THE ICING
140g mascarpone, softened
2 tablespoons icing sugar, plus extra for dusting
    (the more icing sugar you use, the looser
    the icing!)

SERVES

8

TIME TO PREPARE

15 MINUTES

TIME TO COOK

25–30 MINUTES

1. Preheat the oven to 180°C/fan 160°C/gas 4. Grease and line two 20cm loose-bottomed sandwich tins. Using a stand or hand mixer, or by hand, beat the softened butter with the sugar and the vanilla extract until pale and fluffy. Mix in the eggs one at a time, adding a little flour as you go to prevent the eggs curdling. Sift the flour, baking powder and salt and gently fold into the batter, then stir in the buttermilk.

2. Using a spatula, evenly divide the cake mix between the lined tins and, sitting them on a baking sheet, slide them into the oven. (You may have to bake in batches, depending on the size of your oven.) Bake for 25–30 minutes, or until cooked through and golden. Check this by piercing the middle of the sponges with a skewer – if the skewer comes out clean it's ready; if not, put it back into the oven for another 5 minutes. Remove the cakes from the oven and leave to cool in their tins for 10 minutes, before carefully turning them out on to wire cooling racks. Run a blunt, hot knife around the rim of the tins to release the cakes, if necessary. Leave to cool completely before icing.

3. To make the icing, beat the mascarpone in a large bowl until smooth. Add half the icing sugar and quickly beat until combined – do not over-beat, as this will heat and split it with no chance of rescue. Stir in the remaining sugar, then, using a palette knife, smooth the icing over the trimmed side of one cake – add berries, compotes or jam in large helpings here. Top with the flat side of the other cake and dust with icing sugar.

Blackberry and yoghurt sponge

Yoghurt makes a moist sponge and its sharpness works well with juicy berries. Usually, yoghurt would go in place of a bit of butter, making up the fat ratio in the batter, but adding more on top of the other ingredients makes a tangier, more moist cake that is delicious served with even more yoghurt or crème fraîche for pudding – because of the extra moisture, it needs longer in the oven to cook through. The juices from the blackberries bleed into the batter as they are stirred, so that you get little bits of berry throughout the cake. Heaven.

For a larger layer cake to serve 12–15, add half again on to the quantities and divide between two greased and lined 23cm cake tins.

250g unsalted butter, softened, plus extra for greasing
250g caster sugar
1 teaspoon vanilla extract
4 medium free-range eggs, at room temperature
250g plain flour
1 teaspoon baking powder
¼ teaspoon fine sea salt
150g full-fat natural yoghurt, plus extra to serve
a squeeze of lemon juice
200g ripe blackberries, dusted in flour, plus extra to serve
icing sugar, to dust

SERVES	TIME TO PREPARE	TIME TO COOK
8	20 MINUTES	45 MINUTES

1. Preheat the oven to 180°C/fan 160°C/gas 4. Grease and line a deep 20cm loose-bottomed cake tin. Beat the butter with the sugar using a stand mixer or hand whisk, or by hand, until pale, smooth and fluffy. Add the vanilla extract and the eggs, one at a time, beating in a little pinch of flour with each egg to prevent the batter curdling.

2. Sift together the flour, baking powder and salt and fold into the batter until evenly combined. Stir in the yoghurt, lemon juice and three-quarters of the blackberries and pour into the lined cake tin. Smooth the batter with a spatula and lightly press the remaining blackberries on top. Slide into the oven and bake for 45 minutes, until cooked through and golden on top, checking with a skewer. Leave to cool in the tin for 10 minutes, then release it on to a wire cooling rack.

3. When cool, dust with icing sugar and serve with extra yoghurt and blackberries.

Lemon and caraway drizzle cake

NO FRILLS

I can usually make this cake from things I already have. Lemons often sit in bowls, or on chopping boards, or in the fridge with little slices taken from them or half-zested. Milk, just on the turn, makes up for not quite a whole pat of butter. Ground almonds, of which I may have a few or need to buy a fresh pack, make up for less flour and create a more textural sponge. The sugar that stays undissolved in the lemon juice forms sugar crystals that spread over the cake and give crunch with each slice. It's a slapdash, last-minute, loose-ends slice of perfection.

115g unsalted butter, softened, plus extra for greasing
250g caster sugar
1 teaspoon vanilla extract
4 medium free-range eggs, at room temperature
225g plain flour
120ml whole milk
1½ teaspoons baking powder
¼ teaspoon fine sea salt
25g ground almonds
3 teaspoons caraway seeds, plus extra for sprinkling
finely grated zest and juice of 1 large lemon
100g granulated sugar

MAKES

10 SLICES

TIME TO PREPARE

20 MINUTES

TIME TO COOK

60–70 MINUTES

1. Preheat the oven to 180°C/fan 160°C/gas 4. Grease a 1 litre loaf tin and line with greaseproof paper. Using a stand or hand mixer, or by hand, cream the butter and sugar together until pale and fluffy. Add the vanilla extract, then beat in the eggs one by one, adding a little bit of the flour with each egg to prevent the mixture curdling, until well combined. Do not over-beat.

2. Add the milk gradually. Then sift and fold in the rest of the flour, the baking powder, salt, ground almonds, caraway seeds and lemon zest until the mixture is smooth.

3. Pour the batter into the cake tin and level it out with a spatula. Slide the tin into the oven and bake for 60–70 minutes, or until a skewer inserted into the middle of the cake comes away clean.

4. While the cake is cooking, make the topping. In a bowl, pour the juice of the lemon over the granulated sugar and leave to infuse, without stirring. When the cake comes out of the oven, leave it to cool for 5 minutes.

5. Puncture holes into the cake with a skewer and pour over the lemon mixture, leaving the undissolved sugar in the bowl. Spread this over the cake roughly so that it forms sugar crystals (if you don't want crystals, mix the lemon and sugar until dissolved before pouring it over the cake). Sprinkle the cake with extra caraway seeds and leave to cool completely. When cool, remove the cake from the tin, peel off the paper, then slice thickly to serve.

Upside-down plum cake

Depending on your harvest of plums, or what you can buy, try to fit as many halves into the base of the tin as you can – the fruit makes the cake. If your plums are not fully ripe, don't panic. The slight sourness sets off the sweetness of the batter and the plums will be caramelised by the sugar and butter beneath them, the juices blotting deep pink splashes into the sponge. A lovely puddingy cake – and good for breakfast too.

FOR THE PLUMS

30g unsalted butter, softened
30g demerara sugar
grated zest of ½ a lemon
about 8 fresh plums (450g), halved, stoned and
    thinly sliced

FOR THE SPONGE

150g unsalted butter, softened, plus extra
    for greasing
150g caster sugar
1 teaspoon vanilla extract
3 medium free-range eggs, at room temperature
150g plain flour
juice of ½ a lemon
1 teaspoon baking powder
a pinch of fine sea salt

SERVES	TIME TO PREPARE	TIME TO COOK
8	15 MINUTES	40–50 MINUTES

1. Preheat the oven to 180°C/fan 160°C/gas 4. Grease a 20cm non-stick cake tin (not loose-bottomed, as the juices from the plums tend to spill, and no need to line it – the juices from the plums make it an easy cake to release from the tin). For the plums, beat together the softened butter, demerara sugar and lemon zest and spread over the base of the cake tin. Arrange the plums in a spiral, covering the base of the tin.

2. For the sponge, beat together the butter, sugar and vanilla extract until pale and fluffy. Beat in the eggs, one by one, adding a little flour with each egg as you beat to prevent the mixture curdling. Stir in the lemon juice.

3. Sift the flour, baking powder and salt into the sugar and butter and fold in until well combined. Do not over-beat.

4. Carefully spoon the batter into the tin to cover the plums. Slide into the oven on a baking sheet and bake for 40–50 minutes, until well-risen and cooked through, testing with a skewer – it may be a little sticky from the plums but there should be no wet crumbs. Remove the cake from the oven and leave to cool for 10 minutes in the tin before sliding a knife around the sponge and turning it out on to a wire cooling rack.

Semolina cardamom orange cake

This is a classic olive oil cake that should be in every cook's repertoire. The recipe follows the all-in-one method – very easy and hassle-free, no need to aerate hard fats or carefully fold in heavy flour. Baking with olive oil produces a light, juicy sponge with a wonderful aroma, especially when paired with a sticky, spiced citrus syrup. Use an olive oil that you like the flavour of, as you will taste it as it bakes. Semolina gives grain and crunch to the cake.

200ml olive oil, plus extra for greasing
250g caster sugar
100g ground almonds
150g fine semolina
2 teaspoons baking powder
4 medium free-range eggs, at room temperature
50ml whole milk
grated zest of 2 oranges
1 teaspoon vanilla extract
¼ teaspoon fine sea salt

FOR THE SYRUP
juice of 1 orange
50g light brown sugar
4 whole cardamom pods, plus seeds from
    2 pods, crushed

SERVES	TIME TO PREPARE	TIME TO COOK
8–10	15 MINUTES + INFUSING	50–60 MINUTES

1. Preheat the oven to 180°C/fan 160°C/gas 4. Grease and line the base of a 20cm loose-bottomed cake tin. In a mixing bowl, combine the caster sugar, ground almonds, semolina and baking powder. Make a well in the centre, then add the eggs one at a time. Then whisk in the milk, orange zest, olive oil, vanilla extract and salt until well combined to make a loose batter.

2. Spoon the batter into the prepared tin, level with a spatula, then bake for 50–60 minutes, until a skewer inserted into the middle of the cake comes out clean. Leave the cake to cool in the tin.

3. Meanwhile, make the syrup. Gently heat the orange juice, sugar, whole and crushed cardamom seeds in a small saucepan over a medium-low heat. When the sugar dissolves, turn up the heat and simmer for 3 minutes, until starting to thicken. Set aside to infuse for 10–15 minutes.

4. Pierce the warm sponge in the tin several times with a skewer, then drizzle over the syrup through a sieve. Set aside for 1 hour in the tin, then transfer to a wire rack to cool completely.

SPONGE CAKE

Banana, hazelnut and butterscotch loaf

This has to be my favourite cake. It is sweet, lemony and sticky. Whisking melted butter into the sugar and eggs makes a denser sponge, with a similar texture to the bits of banana scattered through the loaf. I like pouring just a little butterscotch over the cake while it's still warm so some can seep in, then pouring the rest into a jug for friends to pour as they wish – which may mean you want to make double the amount of butterscotch … To double the butterscotch, match the ingredients again exactly, but use just 1 vanilla pod.

2 large ripe bananas, mashed (freeze the blackening bananas in your fruit bowl and pull them out for when you make this loaf)
100g unsalted butter, melted, plus extra for greasing
100g golden caster sugar
1 heaped tablespoon chopped hazelnuts, plus extra unblanched halved hazelnuts to serve
1 teaspoon vanilla extract
1 tablespoon dark rum or whisky
1 large free-range egg
150g plain flour
1 teaspoon baking powder (some banana breads use bicarbonate of soda – often paired with cakes that contain acidic fruits; baking powder compensates for the acid already but I think it gives a fluffier sponge)
¼ teaspoon fine sea salt

FOR THE BUTTERSCOTCH
50g unsalted butter
50g soft brown sugar
50g golden syrup
1 vanilla pod, split
a good squeeze of lemon juice
75ml double cream

MAKES

8 SLICES

TIME TO PREPARE

20 MINUTES

TIME TO COOK

45 MINUTES

1. First, make the butterscotch. Place the butter, brown sugar, golden syrup and vanilla pod in a small saucepan and bring to a gentle simmer. Remove from the heat and add the lemon juice to taste, then stir in the double cream. Cover with clingfilm to stop it setting.

2. Preheat the oven to 180°C/fan 160°C/gas 4. Grease and line a 1 litre loaf tin with baking parchment.

3. Mix the mashed bananas with the melted butter and golden caster sugar, then stir in the chopped hazelnuts. Stir in the vanilla and rum or whisky, then beat in the egg. Sift in the flour, baking powder and salt and gently fold through the banana mix with a metal spoon.

4. Pour the mix into the loaf tin – it should come about halfway up the tin – and slide into the oven. Bake for 45 minutes – the cake should be risen, flush with the tin, golden on top, with a soft, moist sponge. Check that it is done by poking a skewer through the centre.

5. Pierce holes in the cake with a skewer as you would with a drizzle cake. Pour over 2 tablespoons of the butterscotch, sprinkle over the unblanched halved hazelnuts, and leave the loaf to cool completely before serving.

Chocolate chunk vanilla sponge with peanut butter icing

This is a outrageously rich cake, smothered in creamy peanut butter icing and dotted inside with odd-sized chunks of melted chocolate. It's the birthday cake of dreams.

175g unsalted butter, softened, plus extra
    for greasing
250g golden caster sugar
1 teaspoon vanilla extract
4 medium free-range eggs, at room temperature
250g plain flour
2 teaspoons baking powder
¼ teaspoon fine sea salt
4 tablespoons soured cream
150g milk and dark chocolate, broken into
    small pieces (or chocolate chips)

FOR THE ICING
20g icing sugar
30g unsalted butter, softened
3 tablespoons smooth peanut butter
vanilla paste (optional)

SERVES	TIME TO PREPARE	TIME TO COOK
8	20 MINUTES	40–50 MINUTES

1. Preheat the oven to 180°C/fan 160°C/gas 4. Lightly grease and line a loose-bottomed 20cm cake tin. Using a stand mixer, hand whisk or by hand, cream the butter, sugar and vanilla together until pale, fluffy and smooth. Beat in the eggs, one at a time, throwing in a little flour with every addition to prevent curdling.

2. Sift in the flour, baking powder and salt and gently fold into the batter until combined. Stir in the soured cream and chocolate chunks, then pour into the prepared cake tin. Slide into the oven on a baking sheet and bake for 40–50 minutes, until cooked through, checking with a skewer.

3. Remove from the oven and leave to cool for 10 minutes in the tin before releasing on to a wire rack until completely cool.

4. To make the icing, cream the icing sugar and butter until and smooth. Stir in the peanut butter until combined. Add ½ teaspoon vanilla paste if you want a little more sweetness.

Clara's marmalade tray bake

GET CREATIVE

Clara makes the best cakes of anyone I know. She makes a sublime chocolate Guinness cake which comes only slightly second to this sticky marmalade ginger tray. She's keeping the Guinness a secret. Slice up into little squares and devour.

250g unsalted butter, softened

250g soft dark brown sugar

1 teaspoon vanilla extract

4 medium free-range eggs, at room temperature

250g plain flour

1 teaspoon peeled and grated fresh root ginger

2 teaspoons ground ginger

4 tablespoons black treacle

5 tablespoons fine cut marmalade,
    plus 2 tablespoons for glazing the cake

1 teaspoon baking powder

¼ teaspoon fine sea salt

SERVES

10

TIME TO PREPARE

15 MINUTES

TIME TO COOK

40–50 MINUTES

1. Preheat the oven to 180°C/fan 160°C/gas 4. Grease and line a 23cm x 33cm rectangular cake tin. Using a stand or hand mixer, or by hand, beat the softened butter with the sugar and the vanilla extract until pale and fluffy. Mix in the eggs one at a time, adding a little flour as you go to prevent the eggs curdling. Stir in the fresh and ground ginger, treacle and the marmalade. Sift the flour, baking powder and salt and gently fold into the batter until combined.

2. Using a spatula, scoop the cake batter into the tin and slide into the oven. Bake for 40–50 minutes, or until cooked through and golden. Check this by piercing the middle of the sponge with a skewer. Remove the cake from the oven and leave it to cool in the tin for 10 minutes, before carefully turning it out on to a wire cooling rack. Run a blunt, hot knife around the rim of the tins to release the cake, if necessary.

3. While the cake is still warm, brush it with the remaining 2 tablespoons of marmalade. Slice to serve.

Three-tier vanilla raspberry cake

There's no need to panic when making a triple-tier cake. It's just as easy as making one layer – you just need to divide the batter between the different sized tins.
I like to serve this for celebratory shindigs. It looks magnificent, but still tastes homely. Raspberries and coconut are heavenly together, but if you don't like coconut, top the cake with extra berries.

The 15cm cake takes 20 minutes to bake, the 18cm cake takes 25 minutes and the 20cm cake takes 30 minutes to bake.

250g unsalted butter, softened, plus extra
    for greasing
300g golden caster sugar
1 teaspoon vanilla extract
6 medium free-range eggs, at room temperature
300g plain flour
2 teaspoons baking powder
¼ teaspoon fine sea salt
50ml soured cream
200g fresh or frozen raspberries, roughly chopped,
    plus extra to decorate

FOR THE ICING
140g mascarpone, softened
250g cream cheese
60g icing sugar, plus extra for dusting
desiccated coconut, to decorate (optional)

SERVES

4–6

TIME TO PREPARE

20 MINUTES

TIME TO COOK

30 MINUTES

1. Preheat the oven to 180°C/fan 160°C/gas 4. Grease and line three loose-bottomed sandwich tins – 20cm, 18cm and 15cm. Using a stand or hand mixer, beat the softened butter with the sugar and the vanilla extract until pale and fluffy. Mix in the eggs one at a time, with a pinch of flour with each addition, then sift and gently fold in the flour with the baking powder and salt. Stir in the soured cream and raspberries.

2. Using a spatula, divide the cake mix between the lined tins – roughly 200g for the 15cm, 400g for the 18cm and 550g for the 20cm. Level out the batter and slide into the oven. Bake for between 15 and 30 minutes (see introduction, opposite), until cooked through and golden and a skewer comes out clean when inserted into the middle of the cakes (you may want to cook the cakes separately so that you're not continuously opening the oven door).

3. Remove from the oven and leave the cakes to cool in their tins for 10 minutes before turning them out on to wire racks to cool completely.

4. To make the icing, beat the mascarpone and cream cheese in a large bowl until combined. Add the icing sugar and beat until smooth and thick. Set aside until the cake has completely cooled.

5. Place 2 sheets of baking parchment or greaseproof paper side by side on your serving platter – this is so you can easily pull the sheets away when the cake is iced and keep your plate clean. Using a clean palette knife, dollop two-fifths of the icing into the middle of the largest cake, flat side facing upwards. Push the icing from the middle to the edges, lift the knife and start again in every direction. Always make sure you have plenty of icing on your spatula before you ice bits that are just sponge, otherwise crumbs will fold into the icing. Then, with another one-fifth of the icing, do the same with next size of cake, flat side facing up. Finish with the smallest cake, and another one-fifth of the icing, again with the flattest side facing upwards.

6. Use the last one-fifth to ice the sides (this is optional – the cake is lovely with just the tops iced if you can't face doing the whole thing). Starting with plenty of icing on your spatula, move the icing around the cake in one direction. You can do this in stages, but never go back on yourself, as this will pick up crumbs. Evenly sprinkle on the desiccated coconut, if you like, and decorate with extra raspberries.

Salted chocolate pistachio cake

Don't be fooled by the no-flour goodliness. This cake is not for the faint-hearted, nor for those with eyes bigger than stomachs – you'll only need a thin slice of this on a plate (and then you'll have a little room for seconds). Freeze what you have left over, if any, or keep it in the fridge for up to a week.

150g unsalted butter, chopped, plus extra for greasing

250g caster sugar

200g plain and milk chocolate, chopped

100ml whole milk

4 medium free-range eggs, separated

1 teaspoon vanilla extract

100g shelled pistachios, crushed, plus extra (whole) to serve (optional)

1½ teaspoons fine sea salt

250g ground almonds

10g cocoa powder, plus extra for dusting

1 teaspoon baking powder

crème fraîche, to serve

SERVES

8–10

TIME TO PREPARE

15 MINUTES

TIME TO COOK

45–55 MINUTES

1. Preheat the oven to 180°C/fan 160°C/gas 4. Grease and line a 20cm loose-bottomed cake tin and lightly dust with cocoa powder. Gently melt the butter, sugar and chocolate together in a large saucepan over a medium heat until the sugar has dissolved and the chocolate completely melted. Remove from the heat, allow to cool slightly, then stir in the milk and egg yolks, vanilla, pistachios and salt. Sift the ground almonds, cocoa powder, baking powder into a large bowl, then gradually fold in the chocolate mixture until evenly combined.

2. In a very clean, dry bowl whisk the egg whites to stiff peaks. Fold the whites, little by little, into the chocolate mix with a metal spoon, being carefully not to knock the air out, until combined (this aerates the sponge where the butter does not).

3. Gently pour the batter into the cake tin and slide into the oven to bake for 45–55 minutes, or until a skewer inserted into the middle comes out clean.

4. Leave the cake to cool completely in its tin, before serving on a large plate with a dollop of tart crème fraîche and extra pistachios, if you like.

Brown sugar breakfast cakes

NIGHT IN

Easily multipliable, good to freeze, and great little offerings. Ready in no time. Make them the night before and gobble them for breakfast the next day.

60g light brown sugar

60g unsalted butter, softened, plus extra for greasing

a drop of vanilla extract

1 medium free-range egg, at room temperature

¼ teaspoon flaked sea salt

60g plain flour

¼ teaspoon baking powder

16 fresh blueberries, dusted with flour

2 tablespoons granola or muesli (or other cereal from the cupboard)

1. Preheat the oven to 180°C/fan 160°C/gas 4. Grease 4 moulds on a muffin tray, and line with large squares of greaseproof paper, if you like – this is just for décor.

2. Beat the sugar, butter and vanilla extract for 2 minutes, until light and fluffy (this will be quick with so little mixture). Beat in the egg, then fold in the salt, flour and baking powder.

3. Divide the batter between the muffin moulds, scatter with blueberries and granola, and place in the oven for 15 minutes, until risen, golden and cooked through when checked with a skewer.

MAKES

4

READY IN

25 MINUTES

Salted caramel crumbs for ice cream

I love adding toppings to ice cream.
One of my all time favourites is Jamie's
simple combination of olive oil and sea
salt, but with a scattering of crushed
hazelnuts, which gingers up any gelato.
Caramelising leftover cake crumbs
does just the trick too. Keep them in
a sealed container for up to a week –
or better, freeze.

50g cake, crumbled
75g caster sugar
1½ tablespoons water
1 teaspoon flaked sea salt

1. Preheat the oven to 180°C/fan 160°C/gas 4. Place the cake crumbs on a greaseproof-lined baking tray and toast for 5–10 minutes, until crisp and golden. Then remove and leave to cool.

2. Heat the sugar and water in a saucepan over a medium heat. Stir briefly to dissolve the sugar, then bring to the boil without stirring – you can swirl the pan, but as it heats and bubbles and clarifies do not make contact with it otherwise it will form crystals and start to seize. If crystals do start to form, splash a little water into the pan and start again. Let the caramel bubble and turn a deep hazelnut colour, then remove from the heat and pour over the cake crumbs.

3. Leave the caramel to set for 30 seconds, then stir to distribute it through the crumbs. Stir in the sea salt. Sprinkle over ice cream or use to decorate other cakes.

MAKES

READY IN

85G JAR

15 MINUTES

Fig frangipane crumb tart

LEFTOVER LOVE

Leftover cake crumbs make an excellent topping for anything from muffins, to large cakes, to bread dough and anything that needs a little crunch. They store really well in the freezer and can be pulled out and sprinkled over at a moment's notice. But really ... this is just a good excuse for making a frangipane tart – it's one of my most-loved bakes for its crisp almonds, sweet dark honey and juicy figs.

FOR THE PASTRY

60g icing sugar

100g unsalted butter, softened

2 medium free-range eggs

150g plain flour

¼ teaspoon fine sea salt

FOR THE FRANGIPANE FIG CRUMBS

125g unsalted butter, softened

75g caster sugar

50ml dark honey

1 tablespoon plain flour

2 large free-range eggs, at room temperature

1 teaspoon vanilla extract

125g ground almonds

1 teaspoon grated lemon zest

4 large ripe figs, sliced into 3

2 tablespoons light brown sugar

25–50g cake crumbs

flaked almonds, to decorate

SERVES

6–8

TIME TO PREPARE

35 MINUTES + CHILLING

TIME TO COOK

1 HOUR **15** MINS

1. For the pastry, beat the sugar, butter and honey together for 6–8 minutes, until pale and fluffy, as though making a cake, then beat in the eggs, one by one. Sift in the flour and salt and mix until well combined. Bring the pastry on to a floured work surface and mould into a disc. Wrap in clingfilm and place in the fridge to chill for at least 30 minutes.

2. When chilled, flour a work surface and roll out the pastry to the thickness of a £1 coin – patching up any broken bits, turning the dough occasionally so it doesn't stick and adding more flour to the table if necessary. Roll it slightly larger than a 20cm fluted loose-bottomed tart tin.

3. Carefully lift the pastry over your rolling pin and drape over the tin. Press the pastry right into the base and flutes, leaving a little extra to hang over the sides of the tin. Trim the edges by pressing down on the tin with a rolling pin. Return to the fridge to chill for another 30 minutes.

4. Preheat the oven to 200°C/fan 180°C/gas 6. Place a baking sheet on the middle shelf of the oven. When the pastry is chilled, line the tin with greaseproof paper or foil and fill to the top with baking beans, rice or dried pulses. When the oven is up to temperature, blind-bake the pastry for 15 minutes in the oven on the heated baking sheet until the sides are pale golden. Remove the tart from the oven and carefully remove the baking beans and paper (they will be very hot!). Return the empty pastry shell to the oven for another 10–12 minutes, until the base is golden – remove to cool and set aside while you make the filling. Reduce the temperature of the oven to 150°C/fan 130°C/gas 1.

5. For the frangipane filling, beat together the butter, sugar and honey until well combined, then add the eggs, one by one, adding ½ tablespoon of flour with each egg to stop it curdling. Add the vanilla extract, then fold in the ground almonds and lemon zest until smooth. Spoon the frangipane into the cooled tart tin and spread evenly on the base, then layer over the fig slices, cut side facing up. Sprinkle with the light brown sugar and top with the cake crumbs and flaked almonds. Place the tart in the oven and bake for 50 minutes to 1 hour, until the figs have caramelised and the frangipane is moist, but cooked through. Cool slightly before serving.

CORE
Custard

NO FRILLS
Vanilla ice cream

LEFTOVER
Portuguese custard tarts

NO FRILLS
Toffee custard with almond biscuits

LEFTOVER
Brown bread ice cream

NIGHT IN
Chocolate brioche custard pots

IMPRESS
Peach and Amaretto trifle

NIGHT IN
Elderflower possets

IMPRESS
Honey panna cotta with clementines

FRIENDS
Mum's hot lemon pudding

CREATIVE
Fennel seed and honeycomb ice cream

CREATIVE
Rhubarb crème brûlée

FRIENDS
Roasted garlic & goat's cheese tart with walnut pastry

Custard

Ever since wobbly school dinners, and being force-fed lumpy, yellow, skin-covered Angel Delight at the age of five, custard has been locked firmly in my food room 101. It was only relatively recently that I realised that homemade custard is actually very edible and nothing at all like my childhood nightmares.

Cooking it from scratch – full-fat milk, cream, vanilla, sugar and eggs – makes a smooth sauce, far from the dodgy packeted stuff. Everything that custard turns into – ice cream, crunchy crème brûlée and tart lemon puddings – I love. It has the power to transform itself into other very delicious things, whether set, creamy or frozen.

This wheel doesn't always stick strictly to the core method. It works in different ways with eggs, milk, cream and sugar, switching the ingredients around and using them in varying order. Sometimes, the custard is thickened in the pan, other times, it is gently baked in a bain-marie in the oven or chilled in the fridge to set it. Have custard at the middle of the wheel, and it keeps on spinning.

Custard tips

- Always keep the temperature of custard below boiling. Cook low and slow. If your custard starts to scramble, place the bowl or pan in a sink full of ice-cold water and whisk vigorously, then strain through a fine sieve to catch any lumps and return to the pan over a gentle heat or in a bain-marie to thicken again. It will thicken more as it cools.

- To check that the custard is done, dip a wooden spoon into the pan and wipe your finger down the middle of the back of the spoon. You should have a clear, stable line where the custard has parted and held.

Vanilla custard

Stir in chocolate, coffee, spices and fruit. It's a great base to have fun with. It's the sort of thing my Uncle John swoons over. He'll stand on his chair and drizzle it from a height over his plum crumble.
I suggest you do the same.

1 vanilla pod
250ml double cream
250ml whole milk
5 medium free-range egg yolks
150g caster sugar

1. Split the vanilla pod lengthways with a sharp knife. Using a teaspoon, scrape out the seeds and place them in a pan with the pod and the cream and milk, whisking to loosen and disperse the seeds from the vanilla pod. Heat the pan over a medium heat to just below boiling. Remove from the pan from the heat and strain.

2. Whisk the egg yolks with the sugar until pale and thick. Pour the hot strained cream mixture over the eggs, whisking vigorously until beginning to thicken.

3. Return the custard to the pan over a very low heat and stir until very thick, being careful not to let the egg overcook and scramble. To check that the custard is done, use the wooden spoon trick (see tips opposite).

4. Strain the custard into a jug and whisk again until smooth. Serve immediately over crumble, or cover the bowl with clingfilm and allow to cool for ice creams and puddings. If needed, reheat the custard in a heatproof bowl over a pan of just simmering water – do not over-boil or let the water touch the bowl.

MAKES	TIME TO PREPARE	TIME TO COOK
60ML	15 MINUTES	10 MINUTES

Vanilla ice cream

If your freezer has space, it's so worth getting an ice cream maker. A well-churned and frozen custard makes the most faint-worthy ice cream, better than any you'll get in the supermarket, and it takes so little work. Using just cream produces a richer ice, but you can do half milk and half cream, or just whole milk. Use this custard as a base for other ice cream flavours – a drizzle of salted caramel stirred through, or some crushed honeycomb, will send you to the moon, once frozen.

1 vanilla pod
500ml double cream
150g caster sugar
5 medium free-range egg yolks

MAKES	TIME TO PREPARE	TIME TO COOK
600ML	4 HOURS + COOLING	10 MINUTES

1. Split the vanilla pod lengthways using a sharp knife. Using a teaspoon, scoop out the seeds from the pod. Place the pod, seeds and cream in a saucepan and set over a medium heat. Bring the cream to just below boiling, then remove from the heat. Strain into a jug.

2. Whisk the sugar with the egg yolks until pale and thick, then pour in the cream, whisking until combined. Place back on a low heat and stir until thick and creamy. Test the thickness with a wooden spoon (see tips, page 258).

3. Allow the custard to cool before pouring it into an ice cream machine. Following your machine instructions, churn the ice cream until just frozen (this should usually take an hour, depending on your machine). Transfer to the freezer until set.

4. To make ice cream without a machine, freeze the custard in a shallow tub and whisk at 30 minute–1 hour intervals for about 4 hours until frozen and creamy, then freeze until set. Scoop to serve.

Toffee custard with almond biscuits

NO FRILLS

No need to throw away all your egg whites when making the toffee custard – they can go into these buttery, spongy biscuits made for dunking. The biscuits will keep for up to 4 days in a sealed container, so make extra and save any you can't manage to eat. They freeze well too.

FOR THE ALMOND BISCUITS

115g unsalted butter

1 tablespoon dark runny honey

40g plain flour, plus a little extra for dusting

125g icing sugar

140g ground almonds

¼ teaspoon flaked sea salt

3 medium free-range egg whites,
    lightly beaten to loosen

30g flaked almonds, to decorate

FOR THE TOFFEE CUSTARD

1 vanilla pod, seeds scraped out and reserved

250ml double cream

250ml whole milk

30g chewy toffee (Werther's Originals are good),
    finely chopped

5 medium free-range egg yolks

150g caster sugar

SERVES

6–8

TIME TO PREPARE

15 MINUTES

TIME TO COOK

20 MINUTES

1. First make the biscuits. Preheat the oven to 220°C/fan 200°C/gas 8. Grease and line a baking sheet with greaseproof paper. Melt the butter in a saucepan over a medium heat for 5 minutes, until golden. Skim any white solids off the top of the butter with a spoon, then strain into a small jug, leaving the remaining heavy white solids in the bottom of the pan. Stir the honey into the melted butter until combined.

2. Sift together the flour, icing sugar, ground almonds and salt, then stir in the egg whites until you have a thick mixture. Stir in the melted butter until combined and smooth.

3. Drop 2-tablespoon widely spaced blobs of the mixture on to the greaseproof paper, top with the flaked almonds and slide into the oven. Bake for 5 minutes, until golden and chewy. Remove from the oven and leave on the greaseproof paper on a wire rack until cool. When cooled, peel the biscuits off the greaseproof.

4. Meanwhile, make the toffee custard. Heat the vanilla seeds, cream, milk and toffee in a pan over a medium-low heat until just under boiling. Don't worry if the toffee doesn't melt in completely. It will infuse its flavour and you can put the bits back into the custard later. Remove from the heat and strain into a jug, reserving the toffee in the sieve.

5. Whisk together the egg yolks and sugar until pale and frothy. Pour in the cream and whisk vigorously until combined. Return the mixture to the pan and slowly heat to thicken, checking the consistency with the back of a wooden spoon (see tips, page 258). Serve the custard in little pots, with the biscuits for dunking.

Chocolate brioche custard pots

NIGHT IN

An alternative bread and butter pudding with boozy, dark chocolate. Naughty little individual pots of heaven.

150g brioche, thinly sliced, crusts removed
unsalted butter, softened, for buttering
    and greasing
1 teaspoon ground allspice
250ml double cream
1 vanilla pod, scored
3 medium free-range egg yolks, beaten
75g caster sugar
100g chocolate (70% cocoa solids), melted
a splash of brandy

MAKES	TIME TO PREPARE	TIME TO COOK
2 POTS	**15** MINUTES + RESTING	**35** MINUTES

1. Butter two 8cm ramekins. Spread the brioche on both sides with the butter and sprinkle lightly with the allspice. Line the ramekins with the brioche, squashing it down, and fill to the top of the dishes.

2. In a saucepan, stir the cream and the vanilla pod and set over a gentle heat. Bring to just below boiling, then remove from the heat. Strain and pour into a jug.

3. Whisk together the egg yolks and sugar until pale and frothy. Whisk in the hot cream until combined, then return to the pan and gently heat, stirring all the while, until thickened, checking the consistency with the back of a wooden spoon (see tips, page 258). Stir in the melted chocolate and brandy.

4. Pour the custard over the brioche – you may need to do this a little at a time, adding more as the bread absorbs it. Leave the ramekins to sit, absorbing, for 30 minutes.

5. Preheat the oven to 180°C/fan 160°C/gas 4. Slide the pots into the oven on a baking tray and bake for 25 minutes, until golden and crisp on top and spongy below. They should slide easily out of the ramekins if you want to serve them this way.

Elderflower possets

Possets are a cheat's custard – egg-free – and make the best last-minute puddings. Heat the cream and sugar to just below boiling and leave to cool and set in the fridge. Elderflower sweetens and gives a lovely floral flavour that goes perfectly with berries and mint. Easily multiplied. Just add the elderflower to taste.

250ml double cream
75g caster sugar
grated zest and juice of ½ a lemon
25ml elderflower cordial
icing sugar, for dusting
a few fresh raspberries, to serve

1. Put the cream and sugar into a pan and bring to the boil, stirring to dissolve the sugar. Let the mixture simmer for 5 minutes, then remove from the heat. Add the lemon zest, juice and cordial and stir.

2. Pour the mixture into two 8cm round ramekins and leave to cool. When they have had time to cool down, cover with clingfilm and chill for at least 1 hour, until set. They'll keep for up to 4 days, covered, in the fridge. Serve with a dusting of icing sugar and a few raspberries.

MAKES

2 POTS

READY IN

1 HOUR **20** MINS

Mum's hot lemon pudding

Whisking the egg whites to their fullest volume, and incorporating flour and melted butter, gives height and fluffiness to the sponge. The egg yolks, sugar and milk form a soupy, lemony custard which separates to the bottom of the dish, giving you an instant sauce to douse the light, soft soufflé on top.

175g caster sugar
30g plain flour
25g unsalted butter, melted, plus extra for greasing
grated zest and juice of 1½ lemons
    (approx. 50ml juice)
3 medium free-range eggs, separated
350ml whole milk
a pinch of flaked sea salt

1. Preheat the oven to 180°C/fan 160°C/gas 4. Butter a 1 litre soufflé dish. Mix the sugar and the flour together, then beat in the melted butter, lemon zest and juice.

2. Beat the egg yolks with the milk and gradually whisk this into the flour mixture. In a clean, dry bowl, whisk the egg whites with a pinch of salt to stiff peaks, then fold into the batter.

3. Pour the batter into the dish, then place in a deep roasting tin. Pour in enough hot water to come about halfway up the sides of the soufflé dish. Bake at the bottom of the oven for 40 minutes, until golden, puffed on top and runny in the middle. Cover with foil if the top is browning too quickly. Leave for up to 20 minutes in the water bath to set slightly before serving.

SERVES	TIME TO PREPARE	TIME TO COOK
6–8	20 MINUTES	40 MINUTES

Roasted garlic and goat's cheese tart with walnut pastry

Not a sweet custard, nor is the custard cooked before it goes into the oven, but it thickens, and puffs, and becomes a scrumptious savoury custard tart. If short of time, use all-butter 250g shortcrust pastry, rolled from a block.

1 large bulb of garlic, drizzled with oil and wrapped in foil
200ml double cream
1 teaspoon Dijon mustard
4 free-range eggs and 2 yolks, beaten
100g soft goat's cheese, crumbled
50g Gruyère cheese, grated

FOR THE WALNUT PASTRY
350g plain flour, plus extra for dusting
100g shelled walnuts, finely whizzed
½ teaspoon fine sea salt
25g Parmesan cheese, grated
200g unsalted butter, chilled, cut into cubes
1 medium free-range egg yolk
3–4 tablespoons ice-cold water

SERVES	TIME TO PREPARE	TIME TO COOK
6	30 MINUTES + CHILLING	1 HOUR 15 MINS

1. Whiz the plain flour, walnuts, salt and Parmesan together with the chilled butter in a food processor, or rub between your fingertips until the mixture resembles breadcrumbs. Bind with the egg yolk, then pour in the water, drop by drop, until the pastry just comes together – you don't want to add too much water or to overwork the dough, as both will cause the pastry to shrink too much when it bakes. Mould the pastry into a disc shape, wrap tightly in clingfilm and chill in the fridge for 30 minutes to firm up.

2. Preheat the oven to 190°C/fan 170°C/gas 5. Roll out the pastry on a lightly floured surface to the thickness of a £1 coin. Roll up the pastry on a rolling pin and drape it over a loose-bottomed 20cm tart case or sandwich tin, pressing it right down into the tin and the sides. Trim the excess pastry by pressing down on the edges of the tin with a rolling pin.

3. Line the pastry with baking parchment and baking beans, filled to the top of the case. Slide into the oven and cook for 15 minutes. Carefully remove the parchment and beans, then return to the oven for another 10 minutes, until golden brown. Remove and leave to cool.

4. At the same time, roast the garlic. Place the oiled, loosely wrapped garlic bulb on a baking tray and slide it into the oven for 15–20 minutes, until the garlic has softened. Unwrap and cool before squeezing the garlic from its skin. Turn the oven temperature down to 180°C/fan 160°C/gas 4.

5. To make the filling, mix together the cream, mustard, eggs, yolks, goat's cheese and Gruyère, then whisk in the flesh from the garlic cloves until almost smooth. Season generously, then pour into the cooled tart case. Slide the tart case into the oven on a baking sheet and bake for 30 minutes, until golden and set. Leave to cool slightly before serving.

Rhubarb crème brûlée

I particularly look forward to the arrival of field-grown rhubarb in April – slender bright pink stalks, stringy and sour when eaten raw but soft and sweet when cooked with a bit of sugar and citrus. Forced rhubarb – grown in the dark – saves us during the winter months and is still just as good. Rhubarb loosens up the custard so that it doesn't completely set, making a good contrast to the crisp topping. Experiment with your brûlée – go for softened pear with cinnamon or add salt to your sugar topping for a salted caramel crunch. Any leftovers can be churned into ice cream.

300g rhubarb, trimmed and sliced into 5cm pieces

grated zest of ½ an orange and a good squeeze of juice

4 tablespoons granulated sugar

2 cardamom pods

500ml double cream

1 vanilla pod, split

5 medium free-range egg yolks

150g caster sugar, plus an extra 3 tablespoons for brûléeing

SERVES

6–8

TIME TO PREPARE

20 MINUTES

TIME TO COOK

50 MINUTES

1. Preheat the oven to 150°C/fan 130°C/gas 1. Place the rhubarb in a large saucepan with the orange zest and juice, granulated sugar and cardamom pods and set over a low heat. Cook for 10 minutes, covered, until softened and stringy, then set aside to cool. Drain the rhubarb of its juices through a sieve – save these for cocktails – and place the flesh in the base of a 1.5 litre ovenproof dish.

2. Heat the cream and vanilla pod over a medium-low heat until just below boiling. Remove from the heat and strain into a jug.

3. Whisk together the egg yolks and 150g of caster sugar until pale and frothy. Whisk in the cream until starting to thicken. Pour into the ovenproof dish and gently place in a large roasting tin. Pour boiling water into the tin, to come halfway up the dish. Carefully slide the tin into the oven and gently cook for 30–40 minutes, until just set. Remove from the oven and allow the baked custard to cool completely. (You can leave it in the fridge for up to 4 days, tightly wrapped with clingfilm, before brûléeing, if you like.)

4. Sprinkle the extra 3 tablespoons of sugar over the set custard and, with a blowtorch or under a high grill for 2–3 minutes, caramelise the sugar until it is a hazelnut colour and is crisp and cracking. Cool in the fridge for 5 minutes to harden the crust, then serve.

Fennel seed and honeycomb ice cream

GET CREATIVE

Though honeycomb takes a matter of minutes to make, it always feels like you're making something special. It fizzes and it swells, like something out of a Roald Dahl storybook. Stirring honeycomb into ice cream is divine, though you can easily make it separately to crumble on top. The custard is infused with fennel seeds to enhance the aroma of the ice cream and impart a gentle flavour of anise. It's goddam gorgeous.

1 vanilla pod
500ml double cream
3 teaspoons fennel seeds
150g caster sugar
5 medium free-range egg yolks

FOR THE HONEYCOMB
2 tablespoons vegetable oil, plus extra for greasing
50g caster sugar
2 tablespoons golden syrup
1 teaspoon bicarbonate of soda

Other favourite ice creams

• Stem ginger and dark honey
• Salted caramel
• Pear and brandy (be aware that alcohol doesn't freeze so well, so use only a little bit)
• Rhubarb and molasses
• Simple lemon
• Darkest chocolate with hazelnuts

SERVES

6–8

TIME TO PREPARE

4 HOURS + COOLING

TIME TO COOK

20 MINUTES

1. Split the vanilla pod lengthways using a sharp knife, then, with a teaspoon, scoop out the seeds from the pod. Place the pod, vanilla seeds, cream and fennel seeds in a saucepan and set over a medium heat. Bring the cream to just below boiling, then remove from the heat. Leave, covered with clingfilm, to infuse for 15 minutes. Strain into a jug.

2. Whisk the sugar with the egg yolks until pale and frothy, then pour in the cream, whisking until combined. Place back over a low heat and stir until thick and creamy. Test the thickness with the wooden spoon trick (see tips, page 258). Leave to cool.

3. Pour the custard into an ice cream machine. Following your machine instructions, churn the ice cream until just frozen (this should usually take 1 hour, depending on your machine). To make ice cream without a machine, freeze the custard in a shallow tub and whisk at 30 minute–1 hour intervals for about 4 hours, until frozen and creamy.

4. While the ice cream churns or sits in the freezer between whiskings, make the honeycomb. Grease and line a baking sheet with greaseproof paper. Mix the sugar and golden syrup in a saucepan and set over a low heat. Without stirring, heat until the sugar dissolves, then whack up the heat and allow the sugar and syrup to bubble until they turn a deep hazelnut colour. Remove from the heat and whisk in the bicarbonate of soda. The mixture will splutter, grow and fizz. Pour quickly on to the baking tray, then leave to set for 10 minutes, without touching, before scrunching up the greaseproof to crumble the honeycomb. Stir into the half-set ice cream.

5. Transfer the machine-made ice cream to the freezer or leave the hand-whisked version to freeze more. Scoop when ready to serve.

Honey panna cotta with spiced clementines

Gelatine is used to firm up the panna cotta; eggs are left out, like when making a posset. You want to heat and gently simmer the cream and sugar until thickened before mixing in the gelatine and leaving it to set in the fridge. This is a brilliantly fun pudding to serve. Wobble wobble.

6 gelatine leaves (I use Costa)
600ml double cream
200g caster sugar
1 vanilla pod, scraped of its seeds
200ml whole milk
2 tablespoons dark honey
sunflower oil, for greasing

FOR THE SPICED CLEMENTINES
6 clementines
1 tablespoon dark honey
1 tablespoon mixed spice

SERVES

6–8

TIME TO PREPARE

10 MINUTES +
SETTING

TIME TO COOK

15 MINUTES

1. Lightly grease a 1 litre jelly mould or eight 125ml moulds. Soak the gelatine leaves in cold water for 5 minutes until wilted, then squeeze out the excess liquid.

2. Put the cream, sugar, vanilla pod and seeds into a large saucepan and heat to just below boiling, so the sugar dissolves. Remove from the heat, add the gelatine to the hot cream and stir to melt. Strain into a large bowl and stir in the milk and dark honey.

3. Carefully place the bowl in a large roasting tin, then pour in ice-cold water to come halfway up the bowl. Stir the mixture for 10 minutes with a rubber spatula as it cools and thickens. Pour the mixture into the greased mould(s) and chill overnight to set.

4. To make the topping, peel and slice the clementines, removing any pith. Place in a bowl and gently mix with the honey and mixed spice. Leave for 30 minutes to infuse, or overnight in the fridge.

5. To serve, dip the mould very briefly in hot water to help release the panna cotta, and turn it out on to a large plate. Serve the clementines on top or by the side, drizzling over the excess marinade from the clementines.

Peach and Amaretto trifle

COOK TO IMPRESS

Trifle may not be everybody's cup of tea – it took me a while, and I still stay well clear of bouncy jelly and squirty cream – but, for those who do like it, there is something about the peach and almond combination that goes oh so splendidly with vanilla custard. A twee and wonderful-looking pudding to serve in small glasses or in a large glass goblet for all to dig into.

1 vanilla pod

250ml double cream

30g cornflour

3 medium free-range egg yolks

75g caster sugar

6 ripe peaches, peeled, stoned and sliced

4 teaspoons light brown sugar, plus a little extra, if needed

6 amaretti biscuits

125ml Amaretto, dark rum or pudding wine

50g mascarpone, mixed with ½ teaspoon vanilla extract

3 tablespoons flaked almonds

SERVES

4–6

READY IN

50 MINUTES

1. Split the vanilla pod lengthways with a sharp knife. Using a teaspoon, scrape out the seeds and place them in a pan with the pod and the cream, whisking to loosen and disperse the seeds. Place the pan over a medium heat and bring to just below boiling. Remove from the heat and strain.

2. In a small bowl, mix a little of the hot strained cream into the cornflour. Whisk the cornflour mixture into the rest of the hot cream.

3. Meanwhile, whisk the egg yolks with the sugar until pale and frothy. Pour the hot cream mixture over the eggs, whisking vigorously until beginning to thicken.

4. Return the custard to the pan over a very low heat and stir until thick, being careful not to let the egg overcook and scramble. Check the consistency with the back of a wooden spoon (see tips, page 258). Set aside to cool completely.

5. Sprinkle the sliced peaches with a little brown sugar and leave to macerate for 30 minutes. Spoon the peaches into the bottom on a large glass bowl or four individual glasses.

6. Crumble in the amaretti biscuits, and spoon over half the Amaretto. Spoon over half the custard. Top again with peaches, amaretti and Amaretto and the rest of the custard. Spoon on large dollops of the vanilla mascarpone and scatter over the almonds to serve.

Brown bread ice cream

LEFTOVER LOVE

I'm sure that the origins of this recipe lie in some rash mistake that then turned out to be something pretty wonderful (a feeling to which I'm sure a lot of cooks can relate). Little crumbs and tears of caramelised brown bread spread the most deliciously nutty flavour through the ice cream, and with it come comforting and chewy bits. It takes a while for guests to guess what you've put into the ice cream but when they find out, they go wild for it.

1 vanilla pod
500ml double cream
200g caster sugar
5 large free-range egg yolks
25g unsalted butter
75g brown breadcrumbs, plus extra, toasted, to serve
pinch of flaked sea salt

SERVES

6–8

TIME TO PREPARE

10 MINUTES + CHURNING

TIME TO COOK

40 MINUTES

1. Split the vanilla pod lengthways using a sharp knife, then, with a teaspoon, scoop out the seeds from the pod. Place the pod, seeds and cream in a saucepan and set over a medium heat. Bring the cream to just below boiling, then remove from the heat. Strain into a jug.

2. Whisk 150g of the sugar with the egg yolks until pale and frothy, then pour in the cream, whisking until combined. Place back over a low heat and stir until thick and creamy. Test the thickness with a wooden spoon (see tips, page 258). Set aside to cool.

3. Stir the remaining sugar with 1 tablespoon of water in a pan over a low heat until the sugar has dissolved. Stop stirring, turn up the heat and allow the sugar to bubble until it develops a deep hazelnut colour. Remove the caramel from the heat and stir in the butter. It will splutter and spit as you stir it in, then turn smooth. Stir in the brown breadcrumbs and set aside to cool.

4. Mix the breadcrumbs through the cooled custard, then put it into an ice cream maker to churn for an hour or so until just frozen. Then transfer it to the freezer until ready to serve. To make ice cream without a machine, freeze the custard in a shallow tub and whisk at 30 minute–1 hour intervals for about 4 hours, until frozen and creamy. Freeze to set, then scoop to serve. To serve, sprinkle over some toasted breadcrumbs and a little pinch of salt.

Portuguese custard tarts

If you have a bowl of custard left over, don't throw it. These sweet custard-filled pastry bowls are a rapid sugar fix and the most moreish of teatime treats. It's worth just making one or two if that's all the custard you have left. Next time, try these with a dollop of apricot jam on top before they go in the oven.

375g packet of all-butter puff pastry (use 200g here, and store the rest in the fridge for making tarts and pies)
icing sugar, for dusting
250ml leftover custard
1 tablespoon cornflour
grated zest of ½ a lemon
a pinch of ground cinnamon

1. Preheat the oven to 200°C/fan 180°C/gas 6. Roll out the puff pastry to the thickness of a £1 coin. Roll it up lengthways like a Swiss roll, then slice it into 12 circles 1cm thick. Roll out each circle with a sprinkling of icing sugar to 10cm diameter. Press each circle into the moulds of a 12-hole cupcake tin.

2. Whisk the leftover custard with the cornflour until thick, then stir in the lemon zest and cinnamon. Fill the pastry-lined tins to two-thirds full. Sprinkle lightly with icing sugar and bake for 20 minutes in the oven until golden brown.

3. Remove from the oven and allow to cool and sink slightly, then release from the moulds by sliding a knife around the outside of the pastry. Dust with extra icing sugar to serve.

MAKES

12 TARTS

TIME TO PREPARE

15 MINUTES

TIME TO COOK

20 MINUTES

Acknowledgements

Thank you...

Claude. Thank you oh literary agent marveilleuse for making *The Recipe Wheel* move, work and flourish. For swooping by on your herb-laden push bike for emergency cocktails and for re-testing recipes without complaint. I love the way it takes us at least an hour of gasbagging before we get onto proper book chat. Thank you for making sense of it all and for constant encouragement.

My brilliant, brilliant editor Sarah Lavelle at Ebury. Thank you for helping my ideas take shape, for your invaluable guidance and for making *The Recipe Wheel* a real and beautiful thing. You were a faithful supporter from start to finish.

Will Webb. For making it all come to life, for putting up with and sticking true to the way I imagined it all. You have an enviable eye for style and colour and have totally transformed bizarre pickled beetroot prints into something awesome and artistic.

Annie Lee and Laura Nickoll. Though we have never met, thank you for your serious attention to detail to make the book readable and, without changing tone, devising slightly more human sentences. Ursula Elliott. For sending copy to and fro and for keeping me on the ball.

My wonderful team at *delicious*. You were unbelievably patient and understanding when I'd come in slightly shaggy from a morning's writing. You have all ultimately made me a better writer and cook.

To my Books for Cooks girls at the beginning of it all.

Friends and family for being fed and for listening.

James. For laughing at me when I screamed that all was lost, and for everything else.

Index